TOP 10 ATTRACTIONS

Essex County Council Libraries

St Peter Port • Guernsey's capital is the finest Channel Islands harbour (*page 51*)

Elizabeth Castle • Step into the past at St Helier's massive fort (*page 26*)

Jersey Zoo • Founded by Gerald Durrell, it is stimulating, educational and a lot of fun (*page 43*)

Seigneurie Gardens • Owned by the Seigneur of Sark, they are abundant with roses (*page 79*)

St Anne · Alderney's capital is a perfect peaceful retreat (page 71)

Hauteville House · The richly decorated residence of Victor Hugo for 15 years while in exile from France (page 56)

Jersey War Tunnels · A veritable underground city built by slave labour (page 34)

St Ouen's Bay · This Jersey stretch is just one of many spectacular beaches on the Channel Islands (page 38)

Shell Beach · Unusual tides on Herm make it a paradise for collectors (page 86)

Gorey Harbour · Mount Orgueil Castle makes it one of Jersey's most attractive harbours (page 45)

CONTENTS

73

74

40

Features

INTRODUCTION

Picture a pristine sandy beach, nestling in the fold of peaceful wooded banks, or open and windswept, pounded by rolling Atlantic breakers. Envisage verdant cliffs rising from a clear, azure sea, where gulls swoop in the updraughts, or conjure up fields the size of a handkerchief, glimpsed over high, granite walls covered in lichen and wild flowers. Or visualise a sleepy harbour, its doughty fishing craft being inspected by a troop of waddling ducks... such images spell out the amazing diversity of the Channel Islands.

Those varied panoramas are forever changing. Coastal vistas are in a state of flux as the tides rise and fall, sometimes by as much as 40ft (12m). At high tide, beaches disappear, marooning offshore fortified islets, while at low tide bays empty like a bath, revealing rocky imperfections as far as the eye can see. Even when the ebb tide adds many square miles to the islands, all this varied scenery is still neatly packed into very small land masses. The biggest island, Jersey, fits snugly into the window of an arriving plane, while Herm, the smallest island on the tourist agenda, is no bigger than an average farm.

Victor Hugo

In 1852 the French writer Victor Hugo was exiled first to Jersey and then Guernsey, where he wrote *Les Misérables*. He described the Channel Islands as 'pieces of France fallen into the sea and picked up by England'.

Yet the islands have every kind of facility and enterprise that you would find in a whole country. For these are, in effect, self-supporting states in miniature, under the jurisdiction of their own governments. Although they are British, and have

Lighthouse at Corbière Point on the southwest tip of Jersey

been since 1066, the islands are not part of the United Kingdom *(see box below)*. Their independent status manifests itself in many ways, but at the same time their cultures are ambiguously linked to the mainland. So, although their police force is independent, policemen look like traditional British bobbies, and while the islands issue their own currencies (in UK denominations), they allow both pounds and Continental euros to be used. They also have their own rules of the road, yet drive on the left as do the British. They issue their own postage stamps and have their own telephone services, but post and telephone boxes come in colours unfamiliar to the British, just as if a naughty prankster had painted them overnight.

These anomalies lie at the very heart of the islands' appeal to British holidaymakers, who feel both abroad and at home, while foreign visitors are likely to see the islands as being

Constitutional Matters

The Channel Islands are British, but not part of the United Kingdom. They owe allegiance to the British Crown, not to Parliament. Although they look to the UK for the purposes of defence and foreign affairs, for internal matters they are self-governing. The islands make their own legislation, which is sent to the mainland for royal assent, and are divided into the bailiwicks of Jersey (including some reefs near France), and Guernsey (encompassing all the rest), each of which has a lieutenant-governor appointed by and representing the Crown, and a bailiff. The bailiffs preside over the states' parliaments, which are made up of elected members who campaign in elections as individuals, not as party representatives. The bailiff of each island is head of the judiciary, with *jurats* (justices of the peace), a *procureur* (prosecutor) and a *greffier* (clerk) in the Royal Court. Though Alderney and Sark are parts of the bailiwick of Guernsey, each has its own parliament and court and, to a considerable degree, look after themselves.

quintessentially British. Indeed, beach scenes with old-fashioned deckchairs and windbreaks would not look out of place at an English south-coast resort, nor would the cosy guest-houses. Pints of draught beer are the order of the day in beamed pubs on every street corner and down every back lane. The food is a mixture of the traditional British – fried breakfasts and Sunday roasts – and modern continental and Mediterranean fare from open-air cafés and bars.

Channel Islands cows

Yet the islands differ totally from Britain in important ways. Low income tax lures many tax exiles, and holiday-makers enjoy the benefits of VAT-free goods. The benign fiscal climate which attracts billions of pounds into the islands' banks and trusts has resulted in unrestrained prosperity. Financiers in suits can be seen talking on mobile phones in smart bistros, and overt social problems are rare. Crime is minimal, unemployment virtually nonexistent and signs of poverty on the spotless streets are few and far between.

A Gallic Touch

Lying just off the coast of Brittany and Normandy, the islands also have a discernible Gallic veneer. Some old-timers still speak an ancient Norman patois, while many surnames and place names are French. Crispy baguettes are flown in

Beauport Bay on Jersey, the island with the best beaches

each day from Normandy, menus are often in French (regardless of the cuisine) and there are plenty of authentic French restaurants. Seafood, by the way, is the thing to eat, especially lobster and Dover sole.

The Channel Islands are the British Isles' most southerly – and sunniest – outposts. Primroses and bluebells blanket the cliff tops in spring, and orchids may appear in Jersey's dunes in summer. Their isolated maritime position makes them an ornithologist's delight, with puffins and gannets nesting on rocky outcrops, as well as migrant birds such as pied flycatchers, redstarts and yellow wagtails dropping by in spring and autumn.

Despite their gentle climate, the islands can't quite offer assured summer sun. So the tourist authorities promote the islands' absorbing heritage – and well they might: the centuries have left a remarkable spread of monuments, from eerie prehistoric tombs to near-invincible medieval fortresses and German artillery direction-finding towers from the time when the islands became the only part of the British Isles to fall under the jackboot. Wartime privations and tales of shipwrecks are recounted in the many island museums.

Meanwhile, folk and other 'country life' attractions recall more peaceful days; farms with tame animals keep the kids amused; and plant-lovers are invited to stroll through greenhouses full of butterflies, exotic citrus trees and carnations.

While all the islands have desirable beaches and spectacular cliffs, there are differences to be found. Jersey and Guernsey run their affairs separately and ever since they took opposing sides in the English Civil War (1642–51) there has been rivalry. To this day, Jerseymen call Guernseymen donkeys, while Guernseymen call Jerseymen *crapauds* (toads), there being no toads on Guernsey. In addition, Alderney citizens are called cows, while Sarkese are crows.

Take Your Pick

Jersey's attributes are outspoken, from the Rolls-Royces of its wealthier residents to the expense of its attractions. While street posters in the capital, St Helier, announce the opening of the latest nightclub, hoardings (billboards) in Guernsey advertise the latest choral society evening – and millionaires are more likely to wear jeans and T-shirts.

Sark and Herm are the islands where the locals go for their holidays. These unspoilt isles are immensely seductive for their lack of cars, tarmacked roads and other modern trappings; returning from them to little St Peter Port, capital of Guernsey, feels like arriving at a great metropolis.

Slightly more worldly Alderney is more of an acquired taste. Its lonely position makes it the quietest of all the islands despite the presence of vehicles.

If you are still undecided about which island to visit, turn to the summary on the following pages for a quick re-cap.

Which Island to Visit

Jersey
Population: 91,000
Size: 45 sq miles (117 sq km)
Transport: Car, bus or bicycle.
In a nutshell: This is an upbeat resort island with some glorious scenery. Jersey has the Channel Islands' best beaches, with mile upon mile of deserted sands, the best sights – with superb ancient castles, World War II treasure troves, multi-million-pound heritage attractions and the famous Jersey Zoo – and the best nightlife for both young and old. The island is big enough to have unspoilt countryside to explore and a wild north coast for invigorating walks. The small ports of Gorey and St Aubin are charming – the capital, St Helier, is less so.
Accommodation: An impressive choice of hotels and guesthouses, limited self-catering, good campsites.

Guernsey
Population: 66,000
Size: 24 sq miles (62 sq km)
Transport: Car, bus or bicycle.
In a nutshell: A sedate holiday destination, this most densely populated Channel Island has a few pockets of countryside, but still has superb beaches, miles of spectacular cliffs along the south coast and St Peter Port, the islands' most attractive town. There's a host of small-scale horticultural and crafts attractions, and interesting historical sights. Guernsey is best placed for boat trips to the smaller islands.
Accommodation: As on Jersey, but also good self-catering.

Alderney
Population: 2,400
Size: 3 sq miles (8 sq km)
Getting there: Direct flights from Southampton and Bournemouth, frequent 15-minute flights and infrequent ferries from Jersey and Guernsey.

Transport: Car, bicycle or on foot.

In a nutshell: A country village cut off by the sea. This gaunt outpost has good beaches, stirring cliff walks, a mass of 19th-century fortifications and the quaint, huddled capital of St Anne. It's the island least visited by day-trippers, thus the most peaceful.

Accommodation: A choice of reasonable hotels and guesthouses, plus a campsite.

Sark

Population: 600

Size: 2 sq miles (5 sq km)

Getting there: Frequent 1-hour ferry rides from St Peter Port in Guernsey, ferry service from Jersey.

Transport: Horse-drawn carriage, bicycle or on foot.

In a nutshell: Europe's last feudal society has just one foot in the 21st century (divorce was only legalised in 2003). Sark has the loveliest scenery of all the islands, surrounded by rugged cliffs and criss-crossed by pastoral lanes. Beaches have difficult access and can be hard to reach for those with children. Day trips are the most popular way to visit, but the island is at its best if you stay.

Accommodation: High-standard hotels, a selection of guesthouses and basic camping facilities.

Herm

Population: 50 (10 families)

Size: ½ sq mile (1.3 sq km)

Getting there: Frequent 15-minute ferry rides from St. Peter Port.

Transport: On foot only.

In a nutshell: Scrupulously maintained miniature holiday island. Highlights are the beautiful Shell Beach, lovely cliffs and views of the surrounding isles. Most holidaymakers visit just for the day: come when the sun is shining. Consider the early morning Milk Boat or an evening meal.

Accommodation: Just one good hotel, a campsite and a limited number of self-catering establishments.

A BRIEF HISTORY

At the august Royal Guernsey Golf Club, the archaeological equivalent of a hole in one was achieved in 1976 just alongside the fifth green: a triangular array of stones, 60ft (18m) along the longest leg, was discovered beneath the gorse. Artefacts found at the dig date back to around 4000bc. The site is called Les Fouaillages, and experts rate it as one of the oldest structures ever found in Europe.

Evidence of Channel Island habitation can be traced back much further, however. Neanderthal teeth have been found in La Cotte de St Brelade, a cave in Jersey said to have been occupied over 100,000 years ago. In those days, Jersey was part of the continent, a peninsula jutting out from a peninsula; it didn't become an island until after the last Ice Age.

All over this small archipelago, prehistoric sites have been found in farmers' fields: these include dolmens (stone slabs arranged as tombs), menhirs (tall monumental stones) and passage graves (tombs reached by tunnel). This is proof that the Neolithic residents of the Channel Islands – who lived here from around 4000 to 2000BC – had the technology to move 10-ton stones as well as sufficient devotion to build imperishable monuments to their princes and gods.

Romans and Christians

Although the Stone, Bronze, and Iron ages may not have left any significant legacy on the islands, in 1985 undersea archaeologists salvaged a 75ft (23m) -long Gallo-Roman vessel from the bottom of St Peter Port's harbour, in Guernsey. The Romans may or may not have colonised the islands – opinion remains divided – but they certainly passed through.

Little news has reached us from the Dark Ages, but it's certain that Christianity had been established in the Channel

Neolithic grave on the island of Herm

Islands by the 6th century. The first missionary to arrive in Guernsey was St Sampson, but he has been eclipsed by Jersey's St Helier, a hermit who lived on a rock in the harbour and was martyred in AD555, perhaps by visiting pirates.

Around the 9th century the Vikings started marauding in these waters. The Norsemen finally gained control of Normandy from Charles the Simple of France, and in the 10th century the sphere of influence of the Duke of Normandy expanded so far as to include the Channel Islands.

Rather more crucial for the future of Europe, the Norman Duke William II (William the Conqueror) went to war across the channel, and at the Battle of Hastings in 1066 obtained the English crown. The islanders kept their allegiance to Normandy, but with this victory began their association with Britain.

England's hold over the islands transformed their nearest neighbour, France, into a perennial threat. One of many attacks was launched in 1214, by a French pirate known as Eustace the Monk, who left a trail of destruction in his wake. But many more massive French invasion forces were still to come. At one time or another even the most formidable forts – Jersey's Mont Orgueil and Guernsey's Castle Cornet – were captured. Life under siege became so cruel that in 1483 Pope Sixtus IV issued a papal bull proclaiming the Channel Islands neutral.

The Civil War

When civil war broke out in England in 1642, the Channel Islands were divided down the middle. Guernsey joined the Parliamentary forces against the king, but Jersey remained fanatically loyal to its sovereign, so much so that in 1646 the young Prince of Wales was able to take refuge in Elizabeth Castle in St Helier *(see page 26)*. There he remained for 10 weeks, surrounded by several hundred of his devoted retainers.

Instant Justice

For more than a thousand years, any Channel Islander has been able to get what amounts to an on-the-spot injunction to stop an alleged injustice against property. The wronged party invokes the *Clameur de Haro*, an ancient Norman cry for help. The complainant kneels before witnesses on the infringed property and cries: *'Haro! Haro! Haro! À l'aide, mon prince! On me fait tort'* (Help, my prince! I am being wronged). On some islands this must be followed by a recitation of the Lord's Prayer in French. The accused then has to await the court's ruling on whether the *Clameur* has been correctly raised. Islanders still occasionally claim the *Clameur*, while local newspapers give advice from time to time on how and when to invoke it. It's usually used in the sort of dispute that blows up between neighbours – for example, when a greenhouse protrudes into someone else's land.

When King Charles I was beheaded three years later, his son was again in Jersey, where he was first proclaimed King Charles II in St Helier's Market Square. Oliver Cromwell, leader of the Parliamentary forces, was understandably annoyed and he decided to neutralise Jersey as a Royalist stronghold. An expeditionary force of Roundheads was despatched and soon overpowered the local militia. Over on Guernsey island, when Parliament took

Guide in period costume at St Helier's Elizabeth Castle

over at the outset of the Civil War, the Royalist governor and his supporters holed up in Castle Cornet *(see page 52)*. Besieged for no less than eight years, they fired some 30,000 cannon balls into Cromwell's St Peter Port.

One of the most effective Cavaliers in Jersey, Sir George Carteret, was duly rewarded in 1664 by a grant of territory in the New World, between the Delaware and Hudson rivers. He named it New Jersey.

Industry and Defence

In the second half of the 17th century peace brought prosperity, which spread from the local grandees to merchants, sailors, and incipient industrialists. Privateering (legalised piracy) and smuggling swelled the archipelago's gross national product. To keep the 'free trade' running, a sizeable shipbuilding industry developed. In fact piracy was such a promising venture that old ladies were known to invest

Local heroes made of sand: Admiral Saumarez and Victor Hugo

their savings in privateers. So much French brandy was plundered that Guernsey was called 'the bonded warehouse' of British merchants.

New fields opened to agriculture, with orchards producing apples; their cider was used to slake a raging English thirst. Before Jersey and Guernsey cows became celebrities, the most important livestock on the islands was sheep. Knitting wool proved such a lucrative hobby that everyone took it up – fishermen and farmers as well as women and children. To protect the rest of the economy, a moratorium on knitting had to be imposed during the harvests.

As tension with neighbouring France heightened in the late 18th century, and defence became a prime concern. Round forts, loosely called Martello towers, were thrown up on all the coasts; dozens still stand. The militia was reinforced, but an incisive French invasion at La Rocque, Jersey, in 1781, totally surprised the defenders. Jersey's lieutenant-governor, caught in bed, surrendered, but a local officer, Major Francis Peirson, refused to obey, engaging the French in a tumultuous battle in Royal Square, at the very heart of St Helier. Both Peirson and the French commander, the Baron de Rullecourt, were fatally wounded, but Jersey triumphed. Although Napoleon fumed against 'this nest of brigands and assassins', France never again attacked the Channel Islands.

Victorian Vitality

During the 19th century the British Government built comprehensive new fortifications throughout the islands to counter the French threat. Two of the most controversial projects were huge breakwaters that still overpower the harbours of St Catherine's Bay on Jersey, and Braye on Alderney *(see pages 45 and 73 respectively)*. It helped that one of Guernsey's favourite sons was Admiral James de Saumarez, who served with distinction in Nelson's navy against the French and commanded the Baltic fleet. None of the islands reached the military status of Gibraltar, but thanks to the Admiralty's plan to dominate the Channel, the citizens began to enjoy modern ports and lighthouses, as well as roads and railways.

With the welcome introduction of regular steamship service, the islands' agriculture turned to more perishable, but profitable, exports. Jersey new potatoes soon became a familiar delicacy in England, and the fruits of Guernsey vineries or greenhouses – originally grapes and then tomatoes – stormed the British market.

Queen Victoria made three ceremonial visits to the islands to inspect the numerous improvements being made there. Today, piers, towers, statues, schools, and streets are still named after both her and Prince Albert. Although Victoria's Channel Islands subjects were bursting with patriotism, few could speak – or even understand – the Queen's English. At that time the islanders communicated in the ancient Norman patois of their ancestors, and formal occasions required the use of French, the only language spoken in the Jersey legislature until 1899. Guernsey did not make English an official language until 1921.

Channel at War

During World War II the islanders endured five years of physical and psychological hardship. When France fell to the Germans in 1940, Britain proclaimed the islands indefensible, the equivalent of an open city. Many islanders, including almost the entire population of Alderney, fled to England, fearing the worst. The worst arrived soon enough, when thousands of German occupation troops swooped in.

A Question of Tax

It's been estimated that the take-home pay for a married person living in Jersey or Guernsey as a percentage of their salary is on average 10 to 15 percent more than in the UK. A flat-rate 20 percent income tax is levied, regardless of wealth. There is no capital gains tax, no inheritance tax, death duties or VAT. Sark doesn't even levy income tax, instead using a property and wealth tax to pay for public works and services. The thousands of companies that are registered on the islands are exempted from income tax, paying just a tiny annual flat fee as tax, regardless of profits.

What's the downside? Well, Sark, for example, has no old-age pension, no unemployment benefit and, like the larger islands, no free medical care. Despite this, many people want to live on the islands. Unless you perform some essential service or can contribute handsomely to the treasuries' coffers, you don't stand much chance. Jersey allows no more than 10 wealthy immigrants a year, while Guernsey makes only high-priced houses available to newcomers.

Hitler not only wanted to prevent Britain from using the islands, but also saw them as a vital sector of his Atlantic Wall. Slave workers were immediately put to work building impregnable command posts and gun emplacements.

When the Allies started winning the struggle for Europe, Channel Islands civilians and occupying soldiers all suffered extreme shortages of food, fuel and medicines. Late in the war, a Red

Liberation Monument, St Helier

Cross ship brought supplies that saved the islanders from disaster. On 9 May 1945, the emaciated citizens gathered to listen to Winston Churchill broadcasting news of the German capitulation. Tears and cheers greeted his words: 'And our dear Channel Islands are also to be freed today'.

At the end of the war, German prisoners were put to work dismantling forests of barbed wire and digging up more than 150,000 mines. Fortunately for all concerned, the German Army had posted *Achtung*! warnings on the edges of minefields, and a particular colour-coded sign, known to the islanders, always designated a field of decoys.

Salad Days

The days of austerity passed swiftly. High-powered greenhouse horticulture developed and thrived, peaking in the 1970s when 9 million trays of tomatoes were being exported annually. Competition for the UK market, however, particularly from the Dutch and Spanish, led to a dramatic decline in growers' fortunes in the 1980s. Flower cultivation and export has since helped to bring about something of a recovery, but by the turn of the 21st century finance had replaced horticulture as the islands' main source of income, responsible for bringing about unimagined prosperity.

With low income tax, a confidential service and a stable political base, the Channel Islands have become known as 'offshore financial centres' – in other words, they're tax havens. In Jersey alone there are more than 50 banks, 33,000 registered companies and around £160 billion of bank deposits – 68 percent in foreign currency. Freedom from UK taxes has lured wealthy British to set up home here.

Short-Break Destination

Tourism boomed after the war in part because of a fascination with how the only part of Britain under Nazi occupation had fared. Marinas and leisure centres appeared, and in the 1980s the television detective series, *Bergerac*, shot entirely on location on Jersey, helped to raise the island's profile.

Today, thousands of seasonal staff arrive each year, particularly from Madeira and Eastern Europe, to serve in the hotels and restaurants. A downturn in ferry passenger traffic and competition from Mediterranean destinations has meant that most holidaymakers now come to the islands for a short break rather than for their main holiday. Nevertheless, tourism remains the second-largest source of income on Guernsey and Jersey, and the primary source on the smaller islands.

Residency is not for the poor

Historical Landmarks

8,000BC Nomadic hunter-gatherers migrate to the islands.

56BC Channel Islands become part of Roman Gaul but there is little evidence of Roman occupation.

AD555 St Helier said to have lost his head to a band of pirates.

933 William I, Duke of Normandy, wins the Channel Islands.

1066 Duke William II defeats Harold at Hastings: the islands begin association with the English Crown.

1204 English King John loses Normandy, but keeps the Channel Islands and enshrines their right to self-government.

1337 The Hundred Years War begins between England and France: France invades the islands a number of times.

1483 A papal bull decrees that the islands are neutral.

1565 Helier de Carteret colonises Sark, setting up the feudal system which has remained in operation to this day.

1651 Castle Cornet, Guernsey, the last Royalist bastion in the British Isles, finally surrenders after eight years.

1781 French defeated for the final time in St Helier's Royal Square.

1847 Alderney's breakwater begun, the most prominent of the many defence measures against a possible French threat.

1852 The French writer Victor Hugo begins his exile on the islands – for three years on Jersey, then 15 years on Guernsey.

1865 Tomato growing introduced in Guernsey.

1902 Battle of Flowers first held on Jersey to celebrate the coronation of King Edward VII.

1935 The islands' first airport opens on Alderney.

1940 Germans occupy the Channel Islands in June and July.

1942 English-born Channel Islands inhabitants sent to internment camps in Germany.

1945 The Germans finally surrender on 9 May.

1974 Channel Islands join the EC (now EU) under special terms.

2008 UK Privy Council approves changes to the governing body of Sark allowing for an elected chamber.

When the sun doesn't shine, you'll still find plenty to do: quayside strolls in the old-fashioned ports of Gorey and St Aubin, VAT-free shopping in St Helier. The large number of first-rate attractions can be almost as pleasurable on a cloudy day. All that might mar your enjoyment is the strictly big-time traffic. If you get hot under the collar, however, take pity on the millionaire at the wheel of the sports car behind you – with the 40mph (65kmh) speed limit and the jams, he never gets the chance to put his foot on the accelerator.

St Helier

Nowhere is the island's traffic worse than in the capital, and first impressions are somewhat disappointing. A power station tower lords it over the large commercial port, behind which runs the island's only dual carriageway. Close by, high-rise apartment blocks and car parks break the skyline.

Fortunately, the cityscape improves dramatically inland. The pedestrianised streets hum with bargain-hunting shoppers, pubs and restaurants burst with convivial drinkers and diners, and Elizabeth Castle, the Jersey Museum and the Maritime Museum rate among the island's best attractions.

Massive **Elizabeth Castle** (Apr–Oct 10am–6pm, last admission 5pm; charge; www.jerseyheritagetrust.org) has guarded the harbour ever since Sir Walter Raleigh lived here as governor in 1600. His queen, Elizabeth I, ordered the castle to be built to meet the challenge of new technology, the cannon. From all the 17th-century extensions you would have thought the castle to be practically impregnable, but in 1651, during the Civil War, a Parliamentarian mortar shell crashed through the roof of the priory, right into the crypt which was stocked with gunpowder, and caused such devastation that the Royalists were forced to surrender. The castle fared little better under foreign attack: when the French invaded St Helier in 1781, it was cut off from the action by the tide.

Tides still isolate the castle daily, when you can only reach the fortifications on amphibious craft modelled on the World War II DUKW ('duck' colloquially). At other times you can walk out along the causeway. The impressive walls, bristling with 17th-century cannon and jumbo German artillery pieces installed in concrete casemates, artfully conceal a whole village of lawns, buildings and a flock of sheep. In the barracks in the Lower Ward, a vivid introduction to the castle's history reconstructs soldiers' living conditions and displays enlarged photos of the German occupation. The superb 360-degree view from the original Elizabethan fortress of the Upper Ward takes in the 19th-century breakwater linking the castle with Hermitage Rock, where Jersey's famous patron saint lived and died. You can take a quick peek into the 12th-century chapel built around the natural stone bed on which good St Helier slept. The story goes that after he was killed by axe-wielding

Visitors fall into step at Elizabeth Castle

Jersey Museum

Saxon pirates in AD555, he picked up his severed head, turned its other cheek and walked away.

Along the Esplanade behind the bus terminal, the **Jersey Museum and Art Gallery** (daily 9.30am–5pm, winter until 4pm; charge) offers the best possible introduction to the island. Downstairs, a Palaeolithic scene describes La Cotte, a cave near Ouaisné Beach where tools and remains of mammoths have been found. Informative displays are enlivened by interactive videos and touch screens. The island's history is brought to life as you peer at a musketball dug out of the arm of an observer of the Battle of Jersey, the sounds of carts rattling and swords being sharpened fill the air. Further exhibits give an insight into traditions and trades: oyster catching, knitting, shipbuilding and tourism in the 1930s, when the Channel Islands were optimistically called Britain's South Sea Islands. The gallery upstairs is devoted to landscapes and portraits by Jersey artists. Top-floor rooms have been reconstructed as they were in 1861, when a French doctor and his family lived here.

Across the square, in the old harbour area, a 19th-century warehouse is home to the **Maritime Museum** (daily 9.30am–5pm, winter until 4pm; charge includes the Occupation Tapestry Museum; www.jerseyheritagetrust.org), opened in 1997. Exploring the island's links with the sea and its former role as a seafaring state, the museum is full of fascinating exhibits, many of them hands-on and interactive, ensuring youngsters are kept entertained. The museum is divided into three sections: the elements (the island's tides, winds and waves), boats (where you can build a boat and sail it in a wave tank) and, lastly, the islanders and their relationship with the sea. The building also houses the **Occupation Tapestry Museum**, established in 1995 to mark the 50th anniversary of the island's liberation. The gallery features 12 large tapestries narrating in detail the story of the German Occupation in World War II. This was a huge community project, each scene created by one of the 12 Jersey parishes.

Until the beginning of the 18th-century **St Helier parish church** was on the seafront, since which time reclamation work has pushed the Channel back about 890ft (270m). Like many Jersey churches, it's had more than one function, as a meeting hall, sanctuary, warehouse, and even as an arsenal.

Just behind is pretty **Royal Square** – a witness to more than its fair share of history. On this spot, prisoners used to be whipped and pilloried, and witches burned. The French

A Jersey Lily

Pride of place in Jersey Museum's art gallery goes to native artist Sir John Millais' *A Jersey Lily* – a stunning portrait of Lillie Langtry. Jersey's most famous daughter was known as one of the 19th century's most glamorous 'women of the world'. She first rocked British society when it became known that she was the mistress of the Prince of Wales. It was unheard of for a society woman to take to the stage in those days, yet Lillie Langtry formed her own acting company and toured Britain and the United States (in her own train); her amazingly ornate travelling case is on display in the Jersey Museum. The 'Jersey Lily', as she was dubbed, died in Monte Carlo in 1929 and is buried in the churchyard of Jersey's St Saviour parish church, where a white marble bust enshrines her famously beautiful profile.

lost a battle fought amongst its chestnut trees: patches on the walls of the Peirson pub are said to cover up 18th-century bullet holes. The golden statue of King George II was erected by grateful islanders, as a tribute for a £300 royal subsidy for harbour works. 'V' for Victory followed by 'EGA' spelling out Vega, the name of the Red Cross supply ship which brought food to the starving islanders in 1944, distinguishes the flagstones at the square's western end – the work of a local which went undetected by the Germans. The buildings flanking the southern side include the **Royal Court House** and the States Chamber (the island's parliament, where visitors can observe the states in session on some Tuesdays from 9.30am).

Central Market

One public building which is always frantically busy is the modern **Main Post Office** in Broad Street. British stamps were used until 1969, when the island inaugurated its independent postal service. The post office has since turned into a solid money-spinner, with thousands of collectors all over the world routinely buying sheets of each new Jersey stamp.

St Helier's main shopping street, **King Street**, and several of its offshoots, have been turned into a pedestrian precinct providing sanctuary from the town's growling traffic. A few British chain stores are here, but most traders are local, and appeal to the tourist temperament with VAT-free, low-duty goods.

For some earthier shopping, try the **Central Market**, built in 1882. Under a high glass canopy, stalls display all sorts of agricultural and horticultural produce – from carnations to turnips, artichokes, melons, and strawberries – as if they were works of art. At the centre of the hubbub, huge goldfish swim serenely in a pool surrounding a splendid fountain. Fish for dinner, however, are sold a few steps away at **Beresford Market**, where you can buy anything from lobster to fresh conger eel, and, thanks to the influx of workers from Madeira, slabs of dried cod.

If you want to escape St Helier's urban stress, head for the beaches at St Aubin's Bay or by the resort part of town, Havre des Pas, east of the harbour. Just inland, the 10 acres (4 hectares) of shady trees and flower gardens of the **Howard Davis Park** are tranquil, too. In the southeastern corner the Union Jack flies side by side with the Stars and Stripes over a small cemetery for UK and US servicemen whose bodies were washed ashore in World War II. The graves are covered with brilliantly hued flowers. The park was a gift of a local philanthropist, T.B. Davis, in memory of his son, Howard, who was killed in action in World War I.

If it's raining or you're looking for something a little more upbeat, take a trip up to **Fort Regent**, towering over the harbour. Constructed in the early 19th century, the fort was part of a major defence upgrade for the island. But it never won any war ribbons, and today looks like a cross between a giant ping-pong ball and a spaceship. As well as comprehensive sports facilities, it is Jersey's answer to a pier, with the latest in amusement arcades, an aquarium, high-kicking shows in its piazza, and an assortment of fairground rides. Most attractions are free once you've paid the basic charge. The old ramparts of Fort Regent still offer the best views in town.

Further leisure facilities are on offer at St Helier's new water-front complex, one of Jersey's most controversial ventures.

St Aubin's Bay

Spectacular sandy beaches, secluded coves, awesome cliffs, and moody, rocky panoramas: Jersey's ever-changing coast-line is captivating.

The vast sandy crescent of **St Aubin's Bay** sprawls west-ward from St Helier. The water is calm enough for windsurf-ing and water-skiing, and was flat enough to be Jersey's tidal airport until 1937, but there are better places to lie on the sand.

Halfway round the bay, just inland from the coastal road, **St Matthew's church** at Millbrook is famous as the Glass Church. In 1934 the French artist René Lalique was com-missioned to create the windows, screens, font, and cross as brand new, original designs. To quite startling effect, he used colourless glass.

On the west side of the bay, the charming fishing village of **St Aubin**, which is jammed between the harbour and a hill, is just the place for a leisurely wander or a harbourside meal. Attractive old houses now serve as quayside bistros, and a few arts-and-crafts shops are hidden up quaint backstreets.

St Aubin's Harbour

Like St Helier, visible just across the bay, St Aubin has its own offshore fort, begun in the 16th century, and ac-cessible over a causeway at low tide.

Noirmont Point, at St Aubin's western extremity, is an obvious strategic strong-point bristling with a host of German defences from World

Sheltered and sandy Portelet Bay

War II. The four-storey-high concrete tower, looming above the huge command bunker, was the eyes and brains of a network of coastal artillery batteries. Its ugliness merely heightens the beauty of its setting. From the point, you can make out one of the island's most photogenic sandy beaches, **Portelet Bay**, sheltered by steep headlands. It's a five-minute steep descent on foot down to the beach.

The tiny island in the bay reflects a melancholy story. In 1721 a local sea captain, Philippe Janvrin, died of the plague aboard his ship. The authorities barred the coffin from Jersey, so the captain was buried on his own little isle.

From St Aubin's Bay you can easily access the quiet valleys that cut through the island. When Queen Victoria asked to see the most beautiful spot on the island she was brought to **St Peter's Valley**, cutting northwest from Bel Royal. The stream along here formerly powered eight watermills, one of which was returned to working order in 1979. The **Moulin**

de Quétivel (late May–late Sept Tue–Thur 10am–4pm; charge), first recorded in 1309, demonstrates every step of the traditional process of grinding grain. You can even buy its own stone-ground flour to take home.

Jersey War Tunnels and Living Legend

Two of the island's top attractions lie off the main valley road (A11). The **Jersey War Tunnels** (Feb–Nov daily 10am–6pm, last admission 4.30pm; charge; www.jerseywartunnels.com), a veritable underground city, was the most elaborate World War II project in the Channel Islands. Slave workers and civilian prisoners who were controlled by the paramilitary 'Organisation Todt' excavated thousands of tons of rock to create a grid of tunnels big enough to hold tanks. The forested hill above the hospital entrance is man-made, consisting of the excavated earth and stone from the tunnels below. The installation, designed as artillery barracks, was converted into a hospital in 1944 but was never used for patients. The tunnels contain detailed reconstructions of hospital scenes – a ward, an operating theatre, and the officers' mess. They also tell of the pain of the occupation – for residents, slave workers (at least 560 died in the Channel Islands) and for the 2,000 British-born Channel Islanders deported to camps in Germany.

If you prefer history jazzed up with special effects, **Living Legend** (Apr–Oct daily 9.30am–5pm, Mar and Nov Sat–Wed 9.30am–5pm; charge; www.jerseysliving legend.co.je) is the place to go to awaken Jersey's past. The focus of this no-expense-spared complex is a make-

Tunnel slaves

Slave labourers worked 12 hours a day on the tunnels. 'There were a lot of accidents and people disappeared', a Spanish Republican prisoner recalled. 'But every time there was an accident the Germans and everyone else did their best to help and to try to save them.'

believe manor house court-yard, beneath the sea. A multi-sensory half-hour show takes you right from Jersey's volcanic origins through to the Nazi occupation, during which a series of three-dimensional hologram characters such as Charles II talk to you. You also get to experience the strength of a gale battering a shipwreck, while a thunderous noise brings to life the bombing of St Helier in World War II. To recover from the onslaught, there is a craft and shopping village as well as street entertainment, go-karting and two adventure golf courses with holes along lakes and waterfalls.

Early tourists at Living Legend

Hamptonne Country Life (St Lawrence; Mar–Oct daily 10am–5pm; charge), accessed via Waterworks Valley, captures the spirit of rural Jersey, from medieval to Victorian times. Originally built as a simple medieval dwelling it was extended in the 17th and 19th centuries with four buildings, some of them still occupied. You can visit the painstakingly restored thatched dwellings, the working cider presses and apple crusher, or see an exhibition on rural Jersey and demonstrations of bygone skills. A 'goodwyf' is on hand to feed you gossip from the 17th-century farming community and there are detailed information sheets within the buildings.

Craftsmen of the modern era can be seen at the nearby **Jersey Goldsmiths** (daily 9.30am–5.30pm; free; www.jersey

goldsmiths.com), in landscaped gardens at Lion Park. As well as watching goldsmiths at work visitors can browse a range of celebrity memorabilia (including Marilyn Monroe's necklace and Elvis Presley's cuff links), purchase from a range of gold or just relax in the gardens among swans and flamingos.

The main road at the western end of St Aubin's Bay cuts inland and climbs up to the eccentric **Shell Garden** (Apr–Oct daily 9.45am–4.45pm; charge; www.jerseyshellgarden.com), where millions of shells decorate the benches, wishing well, windmill, arches, walls and church of this evergrowing family creation begun in 1957.

St Brelade's Bay

You can drive right down to **Ouaisné Bay**, where there's a big, wide beach, backed by a gorse-covered common. Except at high tide, the beach is far less busy than **St Brelade's Bay**

St Brelade's Bay promenade

which joins it. St Brelade's is Jersey's most famous resort. Cafés and souvenir shops line the promenade, while windbreaks and deckchairs suffuse the fabulous, unbroken sands with colour – a traditional, busy British seaside scene, added to which is a full range of watersports and trampolines.

Directly above the western edge of the beach, but a world away in atmosphere, stands the early-Norman **Fishermen's Chapel**. Its simple interior is decorated by fragments of beautiful medieval frescoes, depicting scenes from the Old and New Testaments. In the **parish church of St Brelade** next door, you can make out limpets and pebbles embedded in the vaulted pink, granite aisles. From the graveyard, a sanctuary path, or *perquage*, leads off to a slipway, allowing fugitives who had claimed asylum in the church safe passage to the sea.

You could be forgiven for thinking that **Jersey Lavender Farm** (late May–Sept Tue–Sun 10am–5pm; charge; www. jerseylavender.co.uk), north of the bay, was a little corner of Provence. Here you can wander round the dreamy seas of purple, learn how lavender is distilled and buy perfumes, bath oils and body lotions.

From St Brelade's Bay, a coastal path or short drive brings you to **Beauport**, a favourite among islanders. This romantic gem of a sandy cove, entirely unspoilt, is accessed via a meandering bracken-edged path down the cliff.

Corbière Point

The rocky promontory at **Corbière Point**, the island's southwestern extremity, has always been one of the more popular places for shipwrecks. It is a wild and desolate corner of the island, were gulls soar and shriek above the rugged coast. In 1873 the first concrete lighthouse in the British Isles was built here. It now runs on automatic pilot, so you can't look around, but it deserves close-up observation just for the lowtide walk over the causeway. In a storm, the ocean spray sometimes goes right over the top of the lighthouse, some 135ft (40m) above the level of high tide.

Facing the lighthouse on the mainland, as if in conversation, one of the 1940s artillery coordinating towers has been adapted to control sea traffic as Jersey Radio.

St Ouen's Bay

The 4-mile (6.5km) beach at **St Ouen's Bay** is big and beautiful enough to grace any island twice the size of Jersey. The open sea rolls ashore here directly from America, and surfers turn out in droves to take advantage of championship conditions; centres supply equipment and lessons. Inexperienced surfers should stay close to the lifeguards; red and yellow flags denote the limits of patrolled bathing areas. The safest stretch is La Pulente at the southern end, which is protected from the Atlantic swell.

During Napoleon's time, the British built no fewer than nine defensive towers all along St Ouen's Bay, such as La Rocco on an islet many hundreds of yards offshore at high tide. The Germans, however, also realised that this golden beach provided an ideal target for an invasion, so they booby-trapped it and built a long, reinforced anti-tank wall – now a useful defence against exaggerated tides.

Behind the sea wall are the extensive protected dunes and marshes of

The long sweep of St Ouen's Bay

Les Mielles conservation zone, the largest remaining area of unspoilt countryside on the island. The sand dunes here host many migrant birds in spring and autumn – particularly around **St Ouen's Pond**, where warblers can be spotted in the reed beds – as well as over 400 plant species, including wild orchids, and many butterflies. Some, such as Red Admirals and Painted Ladies, travel all the way from Africa. **The Kempt Martello Tower Visitor Centre** above the bay introduces the area's flora and fauna.

At the northern end of the bay the **Channel Islands Military Museum** (Apr–Oct daily 10am–5pm; charge) is packed with British and German occupation relics including a rare

Enigma decoding machine, military motorcycles and propaganda documents. It is housed in a coastal defence bunker which formed part of Hitler's Atlantic war defences. For a change of tune cross the road to **Jersey Pearl** (mid-Feb–Dec daily 10am–5.30pm; free; www.jerseypearl.co.uk), where you can watch pearl-threading, choose an oyster at the pick-a-pearl-counter (guaranteed to reveal a genuine cultured pearl that you can have made into jewellery), or just ogle a replica of the world's largest pearl.

Inland, the **Battle of Flowers Museum** (Easter–Oct daily 10am–5pm; charge) displays dried-grass floats displayed at the Battle of Flowers *(see page 99)*. These are the life work of one of the festival's greatest supporters, Miss Florence Bechelet. With an acute eye for accuracy and infinite patience, she has constructed scores of floats to take part in parades since 1934. Her best prize-winners – 40 life-sized flamingos, Boadicea on a chariot, and 101 Dalmatians – are on display.

Grosnez Point

At the northwest corner of the island, **Grosnez Point** summarises Jersey at its most spectacular. The sea spray salts the

Grosnez Point

aroma of heather and gorse on the awesome cliffs, and from the Point on a perfectly clear day you can see all of the other Channel Islands: from left to right Guernsey, Jethou, Herm, Sark and in the far distance, Alderney. France lies in the distance to the east.

Only a gloomy hint of the 14th-century **castle** is still standing: a main gateway,

The remains of Grosnez Castle

bastions and a narrow moat. It is thought to have been a place of refuge in the Middle Ages for islanders fleeing from marauding Frenchmen.

The North Coast

The whole northern coast consists of dramatic, flower-topped cliffs, easily explorable along well-marked paths *(see page 92)*. Here and there the granite cliff walls embrace an intimate bay. **Plémont Bay** is a well-shielded beach of wide, golden sand, reached by steep steps from a café; the beach, however, disappears altogether at high tide and the currents can be dangerous.

Cliffs and rocky headlands also protect the more intimate, sandy **Grève de Lecq** – the north coast's most popular and busiest family beach, with direct access and several cafés. Behind the beach, the National Trust for Jersey has restored barracks from the Napoleonic Wars. The North

Coast Visitor Centre here contains explanations on the bay's past and military significance, and an exhibit on the flora and fauna along the coast.

One mile (1.5km) east of Grève de Lecq, the ocean's fury reaches a climax at **Devil's Hole**, as good a place as any to get a flavour of the north coast's stunning scenery. A footpath leads out onto a high peninsula for a head-on view of cliffs under siege from the breakers, as well as a bird's-eye view of the blow-hole through which the sea, when the tide is high, concentrates its rage in explosive spasms.

Just inland, try out the island's wine at **La Mare Wine Estate** (Apr–Oct daily 10am–5pm, Nov–Dec Mon–Fri 10am–4pm; charge; www.lamarewineestate.com). As well as wine, La Mare produces apple brandy, cider, preserves, fudge and chocolates – all of which, of course, are for sale in the shop. Daily guided tours with tastings will take you through the vineyards, orchards, distillery and the chocolate production kitchen. There is also a recently opened Vineyard restaurant for lunch or afternoon teas.

The remainder of the **north-coast bays** are extremely picturesque, each with its harbour, stone jetty, colourful buoys of lobster pots bobbing on the water, rocks to clamber over, and shingle beach – all good places to escape the crowds. Continuing clockwise, Bouley Bay has a steep pebble beach, where scuba divers and anglers share the clear seas. This peaceful hideaway comes to life every July when it plays host to the hugely popular Bouley Bay Hill Climb, in which cars, motorbikes and carts competing in the British Speed Hill Climb Championship race up the steep road from the bay.

Charles' farewell

There is an apocryphal story that Bonne Nuit Bay (Good Night Bay) is named after King Charles II's farewell to the island – 'Bonne nuit, belle Jersey' – as he left for France from here.

A laid-back resident of Jersey Zoo

Jersey Zoo

The main tourist attraction of this northern part of the island is **Jersey Zoo** (daily summer 9.30am–6pm; winter 9.30am–5pm; charge; www.jerseyzoo.co.uk), home of the Durrell Wildlife Conservation Trust. Gerald Durrell, who founded the zoo in 1959, devoted his life to animals threatened with extinction. Ultimately, Durrell would have liked to have seen the zoo close down due to successful animal protection in the wild. Since his death in 1995, the Trust has been run by his wife, Lee Durrell.

The zoo is a lot of fun and a great educational attraction: notices highlight the threats to each species. You'd have to be heartless not to love the gorillas, or be fascinated by the orang-utans cavorting in their splendid playhouse. There are inhabitants as beautiful as golden lion tamarins roaming woodland, as comical as the spectacled bear, as frankly unappealing as Rodrigues fruit bats, and as bizarre as aye-ayes

The crop-rotation garden at Jersey Zoo

in special nocturnal units. The zoo is laid out in 25 acres (10 hectares) landscaped around an 18th-century manor house. Wherever possible the Trust has tried to cultivate the natural habitat of the animals in its care, and the enclosures are generally spacious and stimulating. A moated enclosure for South America's threatened species is the most recent addition, incorporating a glass-domed interpretation centre detailing the role and techniques of breeding endangered species.

South of Jersey Zoo, near Victoria Village, the greenhouses of the **Eric Young Orchid Foundation** (Wed–Sat 10am–4pm; charge; www.ericyoungorchidfoundation.co.uk) hold one of the most comprehensive orchid collections open to the public in Europe. The late Eric Young started a collection in 1958 and devoted his life to breeding new hybrids.

Back on the coast resident geese and ducks waddling on the beach set the tone for pretty **Rozel Bay**. It shelters a fishing hamlet with a couple of appetising restaurants and a 19th-century barracks (now a hotel and apartments).

From the heights above the northeast coast you may see **Les Ecréhous**, windswept islands inhabited occasionally by fishermen. Part of Jersey's bailiwick since a 1953 ruling in the European Courts, they are mostly undisturbed. One incident, in July 1994, saw vessels carrying 200 French fishermen and their families arrive to lower the Union Jack in protest against their government's failure to protect their livelihood. This minor uprising was thwarted by a team of Jersey police officers.

Next, around the unspoilt northeastern corner of the island, is the small sandy strand of Fliquet Bay. From here you will catch your first glimpse of **St Catherine's Breakwater**, a great stone arm thrusting into the sea. This grotesquely oversized pier, nearly half a mile long, dates from the 1840s. The British Admiralty, alarmed at French intentions, decided to make St Catherine's Bay a port fit for an armada. The project was later abandoned as an expensive blunder.

Two small, unfrequented coves here, Archirondel and Anne Port, are shingle at high tide but reveal sand as the waters recede.

The enormous St Catherine's Breakwater

The Southeast

The pretty ensemble around **Gorey Harbour** – jetty, sailing boats, quayside cottages and weathered castle walls – must be the island's most frequently used picture postcard image. The quayside fish restaurants attract plenty of evening trade and are literally overshadowed by Jersey's oldest castle, **Mont Orgueil** (daily 10am–6pm, last admission 5pm, winter 10am–dusk; charge; www.jerseyheritagetrust.org). Built on the site of an Iron Age hill fort, this rugged fortress stood up to several full-scale attacks between the 13th and 15th centuries. The invention of the cannon, however, shattered its invulnerability, and, had it not appealed to Sir Walter Raleigh, it might well have been demolished around 400 years ago. Nonetheless, it served as a strong point as recently as 1945, when Hitler's Germans manned anti-aircraft guns on its heights. A major restoration project has opened up a labyrinth of passages and rooms previously closed to the public.

From the ticket office at the castle entrance it's a climb up 198 steps to the summit of this conglomerate of walls, halls, towers and bastions. You pass through four wards, each defensively independent of the other, to make a breach on the last ward, the keep, an impossible undertaking. There are small but lush lawns and vaulted chapels to explore on your way to the top, from where there is a magnificent view of miles of desirable beaches and Normandy in the distance. If you visit during the daytime, try to visit after dark, too, when the castle is floodlit and looks its most appealing.

Mont Orgueil, Jersey's oldest castle, above Gorey Harbour

A small geographical jump takes you inland to Jersey's most ancient site, **La Hougue Bie** (Mar–Oct daily 10am–5pm; charge; www.jerseyheritagetrust.org). The site is one of Europe's finest Neolithic tombs, dating back to 3500BC, similar in design to megalithic monuments in England, Ireland, and nearby Brittany. A 40ft (12m) high mound of earth, now a grassy hill, conceals a stone cairn, which in turn harbours a 33ft (10m) passage grave, beautifully intact, roofed and walled with stone slabs. You can walk the length of the passage, stooped, to a funeral chamber surmounted by giant capstones.

Two chapels – one medieval, the other from the 16th century (with faint wall paintings) – stand under one roof on top of the hill. They were presumably built to impose Christianity over the pagan site. Don't expect any definitive answers about the site's origins: the Neolithic tomb had already been pillaged by the time it was excavated in 1924. The museum is crammed full of geological and archaeological specimens, including a rhinoceros's skull from La Cotte *(see page 14)*, dating back at least 120,000 years.

The German bunker built in the grounds of the site bears an eerie conceptual resemblance to La Hougue Bie itself. It houses a war memorial dedicated to slave workers in the Channel Islands during the occupation.

In Gorey village, **Jersey Pottery** (daily 9am–5.30pm; free; www.jerseypottery.com) acts as a magnet for countless coachloads of crafts-hungry tourists. Visitors stroll through the factory watching the mould-makers, clay-throwers and artists hard at work. (Plugged into music, the artisans are oblivious to the audience.) It's fascinating to watch how a ball of clay can suddenly become a beautiful shape or a monotone piggy bank be painted into a desirable piece of merchandise. With such painstaking effort, you can see why the plates, wall clocks, lamps and candlesticks on sale are so

Throwing clay at Jersey Pottery

expensive. The Glaze Craze section invites you to purchase your own piece of pottery and decorate it to your design. A further attraction is the Garden Restaurant, offering some of the best seafood on the island, in a pretty, floral setting.

The beach stretching south from Gorey – about half a mile (1km) wide at low tide – goes by the most stylish name of all: the **Royal Bay of Grouville**. Queen Victoria herself bestowed the title. The coastline is rich in 18th- and 19th-century fortifications (some of which have been converted into interesting residences), as well as in wading birds such as the oystercatcher, with its bright orange bill.

The Germans, for their part, chose Grouville as the source of a million tons of sand for the concrete of their gigantic military construction programme. But there's plenty left for post-war throngs of sunbathers and swimmers, particularly at the busy northern end. (It becomes increasingly rocky to the south.)

La Rocque Harbour, set on the island's southeastern corner, is where a French invasion landed in 1781, timing their arrival on a night when the Jersey militia was off celebrating a holiday (see page 18–9).

Defiant Martello towers sit on the furthest reefs of adjacent **St Clement's Bay**. Low tide here reveals a huge rocky wilderness (St Clement's Bay is known as a notorious ships' graveyard). If you venture out rockpooling, beware of the galloping tides.

The ancient salt marsh of St Clement, *Salse Marais* in old Norman French, gave rise to the name of **Samarès Manor**

(Easter–mid-Oct daily 9.30am–5pm; charge; www.samares manor.com). The house is set in 14 acres (6 hectares) of elegant surroundings incorporating ornamental gardens, ponds with swans and a walled garden full of culinary and medicinal herbs. In feudal times only lords of the manor could keep pigeons, and here you can see a genuine *colombier*, or dovecot – a big, round apartment block for pigeons. A beautiful farm courtyard has animals to pet, horse-drawn cart rides and scavenger hunts. There are free tours of the Carriage Museum and garden talks on herb lore. In the Craft Centre, Jersey Woodturners claim to be the only place in the world producing walking sticks from cabbages. Though the leaves are almost inedible, the stalk of the Jersey Giant Cabbage grows strong and long enough to serve as a cane. You can buy seeds in case you want to grow your own walking sticks.

Cattle Country

How now, brown cow? Handsome is the answer, with patches of white on their tan coats, and intelligent faces with big eyes. Jersey cows are small, with a scallop-shaped face, while on Guernsey they are larger (though still petite), with a longer, straighter face.

Other countries put monarchs, civic leaders or heroes on their banknotes, but Jersey has other priorities. Hold a Jersey £1 note up to the light and you'll see that the watermark immortalises the Jersey cow.

The only competition in producing the world's richest milk comes from the Guernsey cow, which accounts for marginally more golden cream. Both islands are fiercely protective of their breeds: imports of milk cows have been forbidden in Jersey since 1789, and in Guernsey since 1819. Jersey's Long Jack cabbage was originally planted on the island as a supplementary feed for the cattle. The leaves, though not quite fit for human consumption, supplied the cows' winter diet.

GUERNSEY

Roughly half Jersey's size, yet with about two-thirds Jersey's population, Guernsey certainly packs it in. As well as all the housing there are glasshouse complexes for fruit and flowers, with often only the smaller fields left for the Guernsey cows. As the westernmost of the Channel Islands, Guernsey tends to be vulnerable to Atlantic gales – as a local museum of shipwrecks illustrates – but there's always a sheltered bay to be found. Try negotiating the notorious blind corners and unmarked lanes in search of a chapel built of seashells and broken china *(see page 61)*, or a grandmother in prehistoric stone *(see page 57)* – and you'll find the real Guernsey.

In addition, you're never far from the acres of sandy beaches and miles of unsurpassed cliffs on the varied coastline. And last but certainly not least there is St Peter Port, the island's delightful capital.

Guernsey's beaches

Idyllic coves lying at the end of gladed glens and sweeping strands behind rocky reefs – Guernsey's 27 beaches will satisfy anyone's seaside taste. And when the Atlantic waves pound the west coast, they reverberate around the whole island.

St Peter Port

From an arriving ferry, this ancient port is utterly delightful. Yachts, fishing craft, dinghies and hydrofoils busily cross paths in the harbour; the pilot, rescue and ambulance boats stand ready; and halyards of moored sailing boats clink as their crews sun themselves on deck. Every view of the town's steep-roofed granite houses and church steeples comes intertwined in a mesh of masts and lines, as if to reinforce the inextricability of maritime affairs with St Peter Port's fortunes.

The busy harbour of St Peter Port

The whole harbourfront has been reclaimed from the sea: ships would once have moored outside warehouses which are now restaurants, and in front of shops along what is still called The Quay.

Until the Victorians built the southern harbour wall, **Castle Cornet** (Apr–Oct daily 10am–5pm; charge, joint ticket for Castle Cornet, Fort Grey and the Guernsey Museum available; www.museums.gov.gg) was on its own island. It has been a low-profile fort since 1672, when lightning touched off the ammunition stores, bringing down the towering central keep. But much of the medieval military architecture is terrifically complete, and the old stone walls are now enhanced by carefully nurtured gardens. The superb views from the citadel explain the presence of German gun emplacements there. With several specialist museums inside the castle walls, you need a couple of hours in which to explore

Cannons protect Castle Cornet

fully. The military minded should enjoy the Armoury's collection – from a blunderbuss to an automatic rifle used in the Falklands' War – but by far the most absorbing display for all is the Maritime Museum. Privateer licences and colourful ships' figureheads are here, as well as Victor Hugo's personal lifebelt and lifejacket, although pride of place goes to a display on *Asterix*, a Gallo-Roman ship lost in AD286 in the mouth of the harbour. An absorbing film tells of its discovery and salvage in 1982. The timbers are currently being preserved elsewhere, leaving you to study a model of the boat and old fish hooks which, but for a bit of rust, could almost be from a local tackle shop.

Try to arrive at the castle's Royal Battery for the Midday Gun. Re-enacting an old ceremony, two redcoats fire an artillery salute to St Peter Port. The uniforms, the gun smoke, and the background of the port make a dramatic snapshot – marred only, perhaps, by camera shake as you jump at the gun's sudden roar.

Probably the most majestic church in the Channel Islands is the **parish church** of St Peter Port. First mentioned in a document of 1048, it has served many civic purposes through the years, including storing fire engines and guns. The interior walls, heavy with memorial tablets, read like a roll call of Guernsey's great and good. The stained-glass windows replace those shattered in 1944 by an American bomb intended for a suspected German submarine in the harbour.

Behind the church, the **markets**, which are 200 years old, have been given a long-overdue makeover. The previously derelict market buildings have been refurbished and new retail space added for high-street names and local traders – to make the Market Place once more the retail centre, meeting place and landmark it used to be.

Fine Georgian façades which line the cobbled High Street and adjacent traffic-free streets are often ignored in preference to the window displays of the shopfronts flaunting the advantages of VAT-free prices. The **General Post Office** in Smith Street sells philatelic material and models of blue Guernsey post-office vans.

The **Royal Court House**, just off the top of Smith Street in rue du Manoir, dates from 1799. The Guernsey Parliament holds its debates in the main courtroom, in English nowadays. From the gallery above, the public can watch the proceedings (which are held on the last Wednesday and Thursday of each month except August).

The streets north of here (around Hospital Lane) are home to the hidden world of finance; only the brass plaques of fiduciaries and trust corporations hint at the wheelings and dealings going on inside.

Above the financial district, **Candie Gardens** exploits a priceless view over the port, Herm, Jethou and Sark – all enjoyed by the unlikely duo of statues of a windswept, contemplative Victor Hugo and Queen Victoria. There is a collection of 19th-century clematis, nerine and irises near the small 18th-century heated conservatories. The park's Victorian bandstand is both incorporated into, and inspired the design for, the **Guernsey Museum and Art Gallery** (daily Apr–Oct 10am–5pm, Nov–Dec and Feb–Mar 10am–4pm; charge, joint ticket for Castle Cornet, Fort Grey and the Guernsey Museum available; www.museums.gov.gg), arranged in a cluster of octagons. This is the place to go for an excellent briefing on the island's archaeology and flora and fauna, and the history and activities of its people. The art gallery's permanent collection is put away when exhibitions are on show.

To the south on College Street is the former garrison church of St James-the-Less, site of the recently built **Dorey Centre**, which provides Guernsey with a unique and versatile venue for music, exhibitions and lectures. The lower level of the centre houses the **Guernsey Tapestry** (Mon–Sat 10am–4.30pm; charge; www.guernseytapestry. org.gg), which was commissioned as a millennium project and illustrates 1,000 years of local history in ten unique embroidered panels.

If you follow College Street south past the imposing Elizabeth College (a boy's public school), you'll reach the Regency **New Town**, at its finest in Saumarez Street. The already colourful façades of the houses, built with the profits of privateering in the late 18th century, are further embellished with brightly painted railings and doors. From Clifton, flights of over 100 steps back down to the shopping centre make you grateful you're not going the other way.

Any self-respecting French person, however, still has one climb to make. Follow Cornet Street up to **26 Cornet Street** (Apr–Sept Tue–Sat 10am–4pm; free), a quaint, old-

Distinctive houses on the climb to Hauteville House

fashioned shop with a reconstituted Victorian parlour at the rear, staffed by ladies from the National Trust for Guernsey and selling home-made jams and fudge, and then continue on to **Hauteville House** (Apr–Sept Mon–Sat 10am–4pm; guided tours recommended by appointment; charge; tel: 01481-721911; www.victorhugo.gg), now owned by the city of Paris. Victor Hugo lived here with his wife during his 15 years of exile on Guernsey, installing his mistress a few streets away in a house to which he could signal from his bedroom. Guided tours set off every 15 minutes round what his son Charles rightfully surmised would be 'a true autograph in three floors'. Nothing can prepare you for the richness of the decoration: tapestries, woodcarvings, mirrors, fabric, and tiles lavish literally every inch of wall and ceiling, each room being a meticulous realisation of Hugo's visionary interior design. Just in case you forget who was responsible for it all, the letters 'VH' are carved everywhere – into shutters, steps and fireplaces.

It was while standing in the bizarre conservatory right at the top of the house that the writer composed such classic

Writer in Residence

The French novelist, poet, and political activist Victor Hugo (1802–85) was granted Guernsey citizenship, but he never learned to speak English. 'When England wants to chat with me', he used to say, 'let her learn my language.' Throughout his life his heart always belonged to France, and he would tell fellow exiles 'The tear in our eyes is called France.' Hugo's exile, imposed by Napoleon III, began in Jersey, but he was tossed out after three years for publishing a letter critical of Queen Victoria. Guernsey welcomed him and he returned the affection. His book, *Les Travailleurs de la Mer* (Workers of the Sea), is dedicated to 'the rock of hospitality and freedom… the island of Guernsey, severe and gentle'.

novels as *Les Misérables*, at the rate of 20 pages every morning. He was inspired, no doubt, by the superb sea views with his beloved homeland on the horizon. Down in the garden below, restored to its Victorian splendour as part of the Hugo bicentenary, he planted an acorn for a tree which, ahead of his era, he christened 'the oak of the United States of Europe'.

Victor Hugo

Just south of St Peter Port along the coastal road is a tunnel complex occupied by **La Valette Underground Military Museum** (daily 10am–5pm; charge), which was originally built to protect the U-boat fuel tanks from enemy bombardment. Much of the military memorabilia on show at the museum predates Guernsey's occupation, such as silk greeting cards sent home by the troops during World War I, as well as examples of trench art.

Slightly further along the road is the **Aquarium** (10am–6pm, Sun until 5pm; charge), with its reptile house, a pool of conger eels and a selection of well-detailed tropical specimens which are housed in an adjacent tunnel.

Around St Martin

Guernsey's most appealing piece of prehistory stands in the most unlikely spot for a pagan monument: at the entrance to the graveyard of **St Martin's church**, a short drive south of St Peter Port. Called La Gran'mère du Chimquière (or Grandmother of the Cemetery), it was carved in the early

Bronze Age, possibly 4,000 years ago, and modified to represent a Mother Goddess roughly two thousand years later. It acquired its crack during the 19th century when a churchwarden broke her in two to end her veneration, but local outcry resulted in her resurrection. Even today, people – particularly brides – will leave flowers or coins on Grandmother's head for luck.

Just east of here, the opulent **Sausmarez Manor** (grounds: Mar–Jan daily 10am–5pm; free. ArtPark: Mar–Jan daily 10am–5pm or sunset; charge. Manor tours: daily June–Sept 10.30am, 11.30am and 2pm, Easter–May and Oct 10.30am, 11.30am; charge. Sub-tropical gardens: daily 10am–5pm; charge. Doll's house collection, pitch and putt and croquet: Easter–Oct daily 10am–4.45pm) has been the much-loved home of the de Sausmarez family since as long ago as 1254, apart from a break between 1557 and 1748. Today's owner, Peter de Sausmarez, munificently opens parts of the lived-in stately home and its gardens to the public. The tour of four rooms takes in family portraits, fine furnishings, and even King James II's wedding suit. A children's railway runs through the woodland gardens, which are filled with camelias,

Stitches in Time

Channel Islanders have been busy knitting since the 15th century. Queen Elizabeth I was in favour of Guernsey stockings, and Mary Queen of Scots wore a pair to her own execution. Jersey sweaters became known as a result of the number of Jerseymen who entered the Newfoundland enterprises at the start of the 17th century. Today, Guernseys are worn by all Britain's RNLI lifeboat crews.

Traditional guernseys are knitted from thick navy-blue wool, while jerseys are thinner and come in various colours. You may have noticed a lack of sheep on the islands; most of the wool is imported.

Sausmarez Manor

hydrangeas and azaleas. There is also an ArtPark consisting of around 250 sculptures that appear in the foliage, on the trees and in the water – a delight for young and old. A model railway and small dolls' house collection also provide entertainment for young visitors.

Beautifully enclosed by verdant cliffs, **Fermain Bay** (no car park – walk from the top of the lane), like almost all the south-coast coves, is pebbly at the top, revealing sand only as the tide goes out. An 18th-century tower and (more modern) tea room supervise the beach, while high above stands a curious white landmark called the Pepper Pot, a guardhouse large enough for only one soldier. From here it is possible to follow the cliff paths that run both north towards St Peter Port and south towards Jerbourg Point. These are the best way to access the dramatic cliffs and delicious wooded coves that make up this exceptionally beautiful section of coastline.

Moulin Huet cove

The South Coast

On the southeast corner of the island, **Jerbourg Point** has the most compelling views on the south coast (those from **Icart Point** run a close second), taking in St Peter Port, Herm, Sark and Jersey on a clear day. From here you can see and reach **Petit Port**, indisputably the most spectacular of the south-coast beaches, with its perfect sands at the bottom of 300 steps.

In 1883, Renoir spent a month painting in the vicinity of the gorgeous **Moulin Huet** cove (a 5-minute walk down a steep path, past a good tea shop) and the thickly wooded valley above. Small and unfrequented **Saint's Bay** (no parking) offers the added attraction of offshore fishing boats.

Like Moulin Huet, **Petit Bôt** sits at the end of a lush valley – known as a water lane, as a stream follows the road, and indeed the café here was once a paper mill. This equally attractive cove receives more visitors than its neighbours because you can park nearby or come by local bus *(see page 126)*.

Forest and St Andrews

German bunkers and artillery lookouts are the most tangible testament to wartime days, but they convey little of life at the time. The **German Occupation Museum** (Apr–Oct daily 10am–5pm, Nov–Mar Tue–Sun 10am–1pm; charge; www.occupied.guernsey.net) in Forest, the best such museum in the Channel Islands, commendably fulfils the gap. Here you can read both an informer's letter and extracts from the fascinating diary of one Frank Barton, and learn about teenagers who tried to escape to France after D-Day. Recipes for marrow pudding and potato sponge tell of civilian hardships, while a home-made bra and hair curlers equally convey the fortitude of islanders interned in camps in Germany. Street scenes from St Peter Port show miserable-looking locals queuing outside the butcher's shop, and a German man waiting to have his bicycle repaired.

The dank and gloomy **German Military Underground Hospital** (mid-Mar–mid-Nov daily 10am–5pm, last admission 4pm, mid-Nov–mid-Dec Thur and Sun afternoon only; charge) in nearby St Andrew appears as it must have done to the slave workers who built it. More than a mile of corridors and halls were blasted out of the rock.

The management have been keeping a tally of arriving and departing tourists for 40 years, in case someone gets lost in the dark, empty maze.

Also in St Andrew, the **Little Chapel** (also called Les Vauxbelets Chapel; daily 10am–noon and 2–4pm) is both kitsch and enchanting. It is a scaled-down replica of the church at Lourdes, and is

German Occupation Museum

Little Chapel, a mini Lourdes

the third in a series of mini-chapels built by Brother Déodat from 1923 to 1939 (a fellow brother added final touches in the years to 1965). Déodat covered every square inch, both inside and out, including arches, ceilings, and even the altar, with broken china and glass, seashells and pebbles – all in all, a stupefying labour of love.

Around Rocquaine Bay

Back on the south coast, the cliffs become increasingly exposed westwards, culminating in **Pleinmont Point**, a glorious Atlantic headland, wild but for television towers and a streamlined World War II fort. More than a mile offshore, the Hanois Lighthouse warns of a particularly dreadful reef. Automated in 1995, the lighthouse was once maintained by crews who carried out month-long tours of duty, provisioned by helicopter. The rocks around Hanois were labelled 'midnight assassins' by Victor Hugo, and over the past 250 years more than 100 wrecks have been recorded. The coast once formed the western border of the Channel shipping lane, but the lane has been moved 10 miles (17km) to the west, so there are fewer wrecks.

At the **Fort Grey Shipwreck Museum** (Easter–Oct daily 10am–5pm; charge, joint ticket for Castle Cornet, Fort Grey, and the Guernsey Museum available), maps, pictures, exhibits, and archaeological finds offer profound revelations about the dangers of the coast, with information panels that tell the gripping stories surrounding the wrecks, which date from the *HMS Sprightly* in 1777 to the *Vermontborg* in 2003. The museum occupies an early 19th-century coastal Martello-style tower in Rocquaine Bay, locally called the 'cup and saucer' because of its white tower which is set upon a wide granite base.

The west coast marks a startling sea change, so to speak, from the cliffy south coast. An endless rocky morass appears at low tide, sheltering clutches of moored fishing vessels. On summer evenings, the setting sun shimmers and sparkles on the water, silhouetting the myriad outcrops, and luring droves of visitors and locals.

Rocquaine Bay is more than 1 mile (1.6km) long, with alternating beaches and rocky outcrops. At its northern end is Fort Saumarez, a strange feat of World War II improvisation: a four-floor observation tower tacked on to an 18th-century Martello-style tower.

In 1995 the States of Guernsey bought **Lihou Island** from the British Crown. Under surveillance of Fort Saumarez, it is linked to the mainland by a centuries-old causeway. The island is only 'open' when the causeway is not submerged – for as long as four hours during spring tides or not at all at neap tides; for details consult the *Guernsey Evening Press*, the tourist office, or the notice on the Guernsey side of the causeway. Other than the ruins of an ancient Benedictine priory, the pleasures of the 40-acre (16-hectare) island come in the form of migrant sea birds, clover and sea pinks, scores of rabbits, and resident peacocks and ducks. The beaches are

Priory murder

In 1304 a servant at Lihou's former priory murdered a monk. He was subsequently slain by one of the Bailoff's men sent to arrest him. It is thought that a skeleton found in 1962 may be the murderer's.

stony and seaweedy. A 19th-century tenant was a seaweed or *vraic* farmer who built the causeway to transport the seaweed to his customers on Guernsey. Visitors can buy souvenir postcards but no postage stamps. From 1966 to 1969 Lihou took itself so seriously that it issued its own stamps.

The Northwest Coast

St Apolline's chapel in the village of Perelle, near the bay of the same name, is a pretty 14th-century church dedicated to the patron saint of dentists. Faint but discernible ancient frescoes are visible on the inner walls.

Just inland, at the four greenhouses of **Les Rouvets Tropical Gardens** (St Saviour; summer 10am–5pm; small charge), you can stroll amongst crops of coffee beans and tea leaves, bananas and pineapples, as well as a selection of Asian fruits that you may never have heard of.

Gardens in St Saviour

Just along the coast, **Vazon Bay** is a whopper of a sandy beach where Guernsey beach boys come to do battle with the surf. This was the unlikely setting for a shipwreck in 1937. When the SS *Briseis* sank in calm seas, the crew easily reached shore… as did much of the cargo: barrels of wine. Locals pitched into the salvaging with such enthusiasm that 'amazing scenes of drunkenness' ensued. **Fort Hommet**, an amalgam of 19th-century British and 20th-century German military architecture, a restored gun site set on a promontory into the sea, provides a panoramic view of Vazon and the whole coast.

Located about half a mile (1km) inland from Vazon Bay, at the other side of the golf course, is the **Brooklands Farm Implement Museum** (Apr–Oct Tue–Sat 9.30am–1pm; charge), a private collection of agricultural implements used in Guernsey over the past 100 years, situated on a working arable farm.

Continuing around the coast in a clockwise direction: roomy, sandy **Cobo Bay** is popular with families and windsurfers. Next along is **Port Soif**, a small, almost circular bay surrounded by big, easy-to-climb rocks.

Heritage, Candles and Crafts

Off Route de Cobo, near Le Villocq is the **Guernsey Folk Museum** (mid-Mar–Oct daily 9.30am–5.30pm, last admission

5pm; charge; www.nationaltrust-gsy.org.gg), set within **Saumarez Park**. Around a pretty stable courtyard, The National Trust for Guernsey has created a Victorian kitchen, parlour, bedroom, and nursery from period furniture and bric-à-brac, and an old-fashioned wash-house and dairy with milk crocks and brass basins.

About 2 miles (3km) along the main road between Le Villocq and Capelles is **Guernsey Candles**, which was originally started with a £5 candle-making kit. Today it's a healthy business with expert candle-makers displaying the intricacies of their craft for visitors. The detailed models are so pretty that the wick is only a formality; you'd have to be a philistine to set one alight.

Just down the road are the old thatch barns and brick kilns of **Oatlands Village** (daily 9.30am–5pm; free). Built in 1892 and recently restored, the Oatlands kilns stand as

Oatlands Village

reminders of the brick-making industry that once thrived in Guernsey and now form part of one of the island's most popular tourist attractions. The Oatlands site also includes several shops, an award-winning brasserie and café, a chocolate shop, a children's play area and picture framers. Popular with locals and tourists alike, Oatlands is well worth a visit.

Grand Havre

A fishing flotilla and windsurfing sails fill the last of the west coast bays, **Grand Havre**. Its various little strands include a fine beach known as **Ladies Bay**.

Les Fouaillages, just behind Ladies Bay alongside the fifth green of the golf course, may be older than the Pyramids of Egypt, but little remains of the original structure. Stones make up a triangle 60ft (18m) at its longest, perhaps patterned after an axehead or flint – or could it be a map of Guernsey?

Just inland, on the green belt of the Royal Guernsey Golf Course, spilling on to **L'Ancresse Common**, golfers have to avoid being distracted by the magnificent sea views and more tangible obstacles such as prehistoric monuments, World War II pillboxes, and Guernsey cattle grazing between the fairways. Two mounds rise above the golfers' 17th green: a German bunker and **La Varde**, a 12m (40ft) passage grave, the island's largest. In the centre of the tomb a 6ft (1.8m) person can stand straight and examine the huge capstones.

Behind, the flawless beach of **L'Ancresse Bay** is the island's best, with cafés and watersports. At low tide you might run out of steam pursuing the sea hundreds of yards down the slope of sand. The towers behind the beach were built in 1778–9, just before the 'real' Martello was devised in Corsica around 1790. The two-storey cylindrical design, though, is similar – nothing fancy, as though modelled on the sandcastles.

The Northeast Coast

The northeast corner is defended by 19th-century **Fort Doyle**. The occupying Germans agreed that this was a good place for guns, so they modernised it. More modernity can be found in the sleek yachts at **Beaucette Marina**, an all-weather harbour blasted out of the island's bedrock. Because the surrounding land is about 30ft (9m) above sea level, the masts barely peek above the nearby pastures.

The most impressive Neolithic site, saved from the quarry-men in the northeast part of the island, is **Déhus Dolmen**. The grass mound rises as high as the surrounding greenhouses, and the dramatically illuminated passage tomb reveals a carving, thought to be of an archer, on one of the dolmen's capstones.

Déhus Dolmen

Bordeaux Harbour, old-fashioned by comparison to Beaucette Marina, is a popular haunt with fishermen and divers alongside a couple of passable little beaches. It's overseen to the south by medieval **Vale Castle**, now reduced to its exterior walls. It was last used militarily by German artillerymen in World War II.

St Sampson

St Sampson

St Sampson is the second harbour of Guernsey, handling bulk carriers and serving as a boat repair depot. Its development in the 19th century was linked to the export of local stone, some of which was used for the steps of St Paul's Cathedral in London. Prior to this time it was a tidal creek – hence the local name of 'The Bridge'. Despite soaring costs the 'Save Our Harbour' campaign vigorously fought by locals opposed to the plans, the old muddy harbour has finally been transformed into a new marina.

The parish church is said to be the island's oldest, and it certainly looks it. It is reputedly where St Sampson himself came ashore, bringing Christianity to the 6th-century islanders. There is a power station on the Vale side (silent in the summer when the power comes from France by undersea cable).

The beaches dotted along the northeastern coast – notably at **Belle Grève Bay** between St Sampson and St Peter Port – are more appealing for rockpooling and birdwatching than for sunbathing or swimming. But from all along the shoreline, both Herm and Jethou beckon winsomely.

ALDERNEY

In Alderney the excitements are still as fundamental as bird-watching and beachcombing. So little happens that the local newspaper appears only fortnightly.

The characters you'll come across in the pubs are a mix of hardy locals and gentrified settlers of retirement age. With few day-tripping ferries, most holidaymakers stay some time. They, too, are a pretty civilised lot, in search of little more than a week of tranquillity. Many are sailors, who arrive from England or France having negotiated some of the world's most complicated sea traffic and tides. The Race, a treacherous tidal phenomenon, separates Alderney from France; along the northwest coast, the Swinge is only slightly less daunting.

Alderney is so small *(see page 12–13)* that the sea is almost permanently in view. Even though there are cars to hire, it is best suited to those who like getting around by pedal power or on foot. A hiker can circle the island in a day.

Alderney's Yellow Perils

The 'Yellow Perils' is the nickname locals give to the little propeller planes that have been operated by Aurigny (the adjective from Alderney) Air Services since 1968. They buzz about the Channel Islands transporting 300,000 passengers a year and providing a vital lifeline to lonesome Alderney.

The planes are mostly Trislanders, just 49ft (15m) long – larger planes couldn't land on Alderney's runway. There are no refreshments on board, as the planes do not have stewards or aisles, but Aurigny's in-flight magazine contains a diagram of the instrument panel, for back-seat drivers. Aurigny's planes have become a Channel Island institution.

In 2003 the States of Guernsey bought the airline to ensure the future of its Gatwick to Guernsey airlink.

St Anne's quiet streets

St Anne

Alderney's capital, more often called 'town', is, surprisingly, not a port. It was established in the centre of the island for the reason that local farmers wanted to live close to their fields. Some street names are French, but the Norman patois has died out and English is the only language. St Anne lacks stirring monuments (a cattle trough stands in the centre of the main square), but the overall effect is thoroughly engaging, with pastel-coloured houses lining cobbled streets.

Victoria Street, which was named rue de Grosnez until a royal visit in 1854, is the main shopping street. It is a daytime hive of activity but usually eerily quiet in the evening. Here you'll find the whole range of shops and services that allows Alderney to be self-sufficient, post office included, where you can buy the island's own beautiful stamps.

On a hillside just off the street, the **parish church** is almost as august as a cathedral. When built in the 19th century, no fund-raising drives were required: it was a gift from the Reverend John Le Mesurier, son of the island's last hereditary governor.

New Street was renamed **Queen Elizabeth II Street** by the royalist islanders after her majesty dropped by in 1978. The States of Alderney meet in the court house here. As part of the Bailiwick of Guernsey, the island does not have control of its own budget, but is nevertheless autonomous in almost all other matters.

In High Street, perpendicular to Victoria Street, **Alderney Museum** (Apr–Oct Mon–Fri 10am–noon and 2–4pm, Sat–Sun 10am–noon; charge) occupies an 18th-century schoolhouse. It is surprisingly large, and the best place to buy literature about the island. Amongst the fascinating odds and ends covering everything from archaeology to butterflies, there are absorbing finds from an Elizabethan wreck that was recently discovered below the Race off the northeast coast: 16th-century stirrups, the sole of a shoe, and 'apostles' – small brass flasks used for holding a single charge of gunpowder.

Almost the entire population of Alderney was evacuated before the Nazi occupation. One of the most intriguing stories told in the museum concerns the islanders' return to Alderney after the war. At that time a British judge decided their furniture should be redistributed simply by dropping the rope surrounding the compound where it was being stored and letting everyone grab what they could.

In the shadow of Alderney's ugliest war relic, Les Mouriaux tower (a mixture of water tower, lookout and communications post) is an unorthodox crafts centre, **Alderney Pottery** (Mon–Fri 9am–5pm, Sat 9am–1pm). Founded in 1962, it produces hand-made pottery from Devon and Dorset clay. In addition, wool is hand-spun here and made into individually designed rugs and sweaters.

Braye Harbour

Situated in the island's biggest bay, **Braye Harbour** is hidden behind a hideous Victorian jetty that mitigates northwesterly gales. The Braye Harbour project, started in 1847, was immensely costly and only partly successful. The breakwater, which was originally nearly a mile long, still needs repairing after every really big storm, costing around £500,000 a year; its maintenance forms Guernsey's contribution to the British defence budget. The construction of the ring of Victorian forts to protect the incipient naval base all fizzled out after about 30 booming years.

Fishing boats at Braye Harbour

Before the Royal Navy discovered Braye, it was a busy enough little port, much frequented by smugglers and privateers. The cellars of some of the 18th-century houses near the port were used for storing contraband. Today, as restaurants and bars, these houses hum with the sound of tall stories from the innumerable newly arrived yachtspeople. The best-known haunt is **The Divers Inn**, a no-frills place where fresh sand is laid on the floor each day.

Millions of tons of stone were needed to build the Braye breakwater, with a railway laid between the quarries and the port. Nowadays, the **Alderney Railway** is back in business, but for tourists and not locals. Enthusiasts run a steam engine

Mannez Lighthouse

and a more modern diesel from the Braye Road Station to the Mannez Quarry and back, a round trip taking half an hour. It's the last railway in the Channel Islands.

Around the Island

Beyond St Anne and Braye, the island is barely populated. The interior is wind-swept and largely treeless, with agricultural land concentrated in the southwestern corner in hedgeless fields. The varied coastline provides the entertainment. Gently sloping sandy **Braye Bay** is an ideal bathing beach. **Fort Albert**, settled into the hilltop at the east end of the bay, was built in the 1840s as the key fort in the network of British defences facing a presumed threat from France. It has now fallen into disrepair and cannot be explored.

Without local inhabitants around, the Germans were able to devote themselves to developing the island as one big military base and prison camp. Inland, just east of the fort, a **memorial** indicates the range of backgrounds of the slave workers – Polish, Russian, Hebrew, French and Spanish – who perished here during the war. Overwork, beatings from guards, and a starvation diet contributed to the deaths of hundreds of forced labourers and prisoners.

Two other good, sandy beaches are **Corblets Bay** and **Saye Bay** (pronounced 'soy'). Among the many shipwrecks to enter local folklore is the French sailing ship *Carioca*, lost on the rocks near here in 1866. A shipment of pianos drifted ashore. To the south looms a three-storey naval direction-finder tower left over from the time of the German occupation. The locals call it the Odeon.

Situated at the eastern end of the island at Quesnard Point is Alderney's most prominent landmark, the **Mannez Lighthouse** (or Alderney Lighthouse). All of 109ft (32m) high and painted with distinctive black and white bands, the lighthouse was built in 1912 – rather late in the day considering the number of shipwrecks along this perilous coast. It was automated in 1997, and it is possible to take conducted tours with the warden in the summer months.

Longis Bay is a broad crescent of sand and low-lying rock offering safe bathing. The vast wall, erected courtesy of the Germans, was one big tank trap erected to dissuade the Allies from using this inviting invasion route.

Far below **Essex Castle**, a 16th-century fort subdivided into fashionable apartments, is a natural phenomenon known as **Hanging Rock**. An island legend tells how the devil inspired the mischievous Guernseymen to tie their boat to this tooth of stone and try to tow Alderney home. The rock tilted but they didn't succeed.

Longis Bay

Rugged Cliffs

Almost sheer **cliffs** form the coastline from here westward to Hannaine Bay, just about halfway round the

Alderney gannets

The offshore rocks of Les Etacs are home to gannets, the biggest of British seabirds. They nest beak to beak covering the rocks in a white layer, and the air is filled with soaring birds returning from fishing trips.

island. This is Alderney at its most beautiful and ruggedly spectacular. Paths among thrift, sea campion and broom follow the line of the clifftops, and you may see birds of prey soaring in the updraughts. Victorian military planners considered the south coast invulnerable, but the Germans still installed a full quota of bunkers. Hikers are warned to look out for concealed dugouts, tunnels and barbed wire. South of the airport, steps (with a warning sign) lead down to turquoise waters and the delightful sandy cove of **Telegraph Bay**. A concrete causeway dating from 1942 leads out to Les Etacs and another islet, home to **Fort Clonque**, a bouncily christened Victorian strongpoint now available to rent from the Landmark Trust for that ultimate getaway holiday (see page 134 for details).

Rather than investigate the rest of the forts and the couple of scrubby beaches on the completion of the island's circuit back to Braye, you'd do better to sign up for a two-hour **boat trip** that goes right around Alderney. Sometimes the excursions include a side trip to **Burhou**, a couple of miles offshore. This negligible island provides refuge for a colony of funny-faced puffins (though their numbers are declining). Serious bird-watchers can arrange to stay overnight in a basic hut.

Some 7 miles (11km) west of Alderney is the lighthouse on **Les Casquets** reef, where during the 19th century one family stayed 19 years without a break. According to one contemporary account, an artisan sent to the rock to carry out repairs fell in love with the keeper's daughter. He invited her to visit him in Alderney, and she eventually did. But she soon rushed back to the Casquets; Alderney was too noisy.

SARK

Wrapped in a 300ft (91m) wall of rock that rises out of the sea, Sark appears a forbidding place. How untrue. On top of the cliffs, the island's plateau is a botanical paradise, where the hedgerows are festooned with buttercups and butterflies, gardens are heavy with honeysuckle, and flowers perfume the tawny-coloured lanes.

This pastoral sanctuary is, for once, enhanced by human habitation. The meadows provide the setting for pre-industrial scenes of champing shire horses and milk churns being loaded on to carts. This is an island not only without an airport, but one which has banned planes from flying less than 2,000ft (610m) overhead. With the exception of tractors, motorised transport is forbidden, and there are no tarmacked roads. Visitors can tour the island by horse-drawn carriage *(see page 118)*, hired bicycle, or on foot. If you're going under your own steam, you'll need a good map to contemplate all the winding, unmarked paths.

The morning arrival of a thousand-strong flood of day-trippers in summer can mar this paradise, but if you head away from the village, tranquillity is assured. If possible, stay at least a night in one of

Creux Harbour

(see page 135)

Feudal Sark

Sark is a feudal state, run under laws decreed by Elizabeth I in the 16th century. The island was colonised in 1565 by Helier de Carteret, the first Seigneur (lord) of Sark, who divided it among 40 tenants. Today, the tenants join 12 elected deputies in running a parliament called the Chief Pleas.

the excellent hotels or simple guesthouses *(see page 135)*. First thing in the morning, when the dew still lies on the fields, the carts are getting a spit and polish, and the horses are being groomed, the island is quite magical. And while everyone nods or bids a hello to everyone else on Sark, as a guest the Sarkese give you a special welcome.

Sark's prettiest little port, full of plush yachts and colourful fishing boats and backed by a diminutive shingle beach, is **Creux Harbour**. Most visitors don't actually arrive here but at the modern harbour of **La Maseline**, just a few yards up the coast and linked to Le Creux by tunnels through the surrounding cliffs. From Le Creux or La Maseline it's a steep haul of around a half a mile (1km) to the village, but the trip is eased by the tractor-drawn buses that meet the boats.

The Village

The haphazardly arranged village of Sark centres on **The Avenue**, a pleasantly scruffy line of huts with a couple of banks, a post office, a few souvenir shops and a grocery store (good for picnics). At the harbour end of The Avenue at **La Collinette**, horses and pristine carriages stand by. Some drivers are Sarkese, but many are young horse enthusiasts over from the UK for the season; they have to pass a driving test.

At the other end of The Avenue, the island **prison**, with two cells, looks to all the world like a public lavatory. To this day it is sometimes put to use as a temporary lock-up. Two part-time constables maintain Sark's law and order.

A busy day on The Avenue

St Peter's church, nearby, has a pew reserved for prisoners, identifiable by a crossed keys design on the cushion covers. Indeed, the whole of the early 19th-century church is brought to life by its tapestried seating, each pew showing the coats of arms of a feudal family.

Continuing north you come to **La Seigneurie**. Sark's most impressive structure has been the home of the island's rulers since 1730. Though the lord of the manor doesn't invite you to tea, he does let you visit his grounds, the **Seigneurie Gardens** (Easter–Oct Mon–Fri 10am–5pm, July and Aug also Sat 10am–4pm; charge). High walls keep out the salty winds to the benefit of the delightful formal gardens, abundant with roses. You also get a good look at the curious architectural medley of the grand old granite house. At the rear is a bronze cannon inscribed as a gift from Elizabeth I to the first Seigneur, and fan-tailed pigeons nosing out on the ledges of the rocket-shaped *colombier* or dovecot,

Seigneurie Gardens

which is still the only one allowed on the island under the feudal regime.

Today's Seigneur, Michael Beaumount, is an engineer by trade. He inherited his domain on the death of his grandmother, Dame Sibyl Hathaway. Her finest hour came during World War II when, with her unflappable aristocratic manner and serviceable German, she faced down the occupation authorities and defended the rights of her people. She had also learnt *Sercqais*, the Norman-French patois still heard among older islanders. During the war locals infuriated the occupying forces by communicating in this 'secret' language.

On rue Lucas, not far from La Collinette, the **Sark Occupation and Heritage Museum** (Easter–end of Oct 10am–5.30pm; charge) shows photographs of the dame in her prime dealing with her unwelcome guests. Among the many other military pieces (not just from Sark) are a home-made radio (known as the cat's whiskers), German barbed wire, and land mines found on the island.

Around the Island

Sark comes into its element when you leave the village. To a certain extent it doesn't matter where you go, since everywhere the countryside and the sheer cliffs are lovely. Though there are beaches on which to chill out, if you're here for only a day the island is too beautiful to spend it all just lying in the sun. Although it's an adventurous scramble to almost all of the beaches, the climb down through ferns, bluebells, and primroses is an essential part of the Sark experience.

Close to the occupation museum, a lane leads to the **lighthouse**, hunched halfway down a cliffside at Pointe Robert on the east coast. After more than 80 years of being manned by lighthousemen, it was automated in 1993.

Port du Moulin, behind the Seigneurie on the west coast, is a shingle beach far below precipitous cliffs. The coastal views from the top are some of the island's most impressive, especially the outlook through the artificially bored 'Window in the Rock' – likely to cause some dizziness even for those who don't suffer from vertigo.

To the south, the **Pilcher Monument**, an obelisk on the cliffs high above the old-time fishermen's harbour of Havre Gosselin, commemorates one of countless shipwrecks. From this vantage point you can easily survey the private island of

Pointe Robert Lighthouse

Brecqhou. The publicity-shunning owners of the *Telegraph*, the Barclay twins, bought the 160-acre (65-hectare) islet for more than £2 million and built a marble Gothic castle complete with helipad and a new harbour. The twins have donated a considerable sum towards rebuilding the Sark school.

In Sark's southeast corner lie the best beaches, and some splendid cliff scenery from the spectacular rocky spines of the Hog's Back and Pointe Derrible. **Dixcart Bay**, divided by an arch of rock, is reached past the Dixcart Hotel and is accessible even to pushchairs. It's safe and sandy, like **Derrible Bay**, which is, however, inaccessible during high tide.

Little Sark

Sark is essentially two islands connected by a narrow isthmus known as **La Coupée**. Crossing from Great Sark to Little Sark over this natural bridge is an adventure in itself. In 1945 German prisoners of war built a causeway, which now resembles the Great Wall of China, if only 450ft (137m) long. From the middle of it there's more heart-stopping scenery. Cliffs fall for more than 250ft (76m), but solid railings give a sense of security as you take in the view of Guernsey, Jersey and Normandy on the horizon. **Grande Grève**, over on the western side, is a big sandy bay suitable for children, but a long climb down.

Driving across La Coupée

Little Sark is even more tranquil than the main island, so quiet you can hear the cows chewing the cud. Towards the southern end, the remains of a number of outsized stone chimney pots erupt on the ground as melancholy monuments to a **silver mining** venture of the 19th century. Though the plan looked promising on paper, no viable quantities of any mineral were found. One shaft, burrowed deep under the sea, was flooded in 1845, drowning ten miners and sinking the project.

Few make it as far as the southern tip of Little Sark and **Venus Pool**, a rock pool where the deep, clear water is replenished with every tide. If heaven were to come in the form of lonesome cliffscapes, it could well look like this.

HERM

Sark may have no cars, but diminutive Herm goes one better: but for the local children's, it doesn't even allow bicycles. Though situated just 3 miles (5km) and a 20-minute ferry ride from the metropolis of St Peter Port, Herm is the Channel Islands' peerless getaway holiday island.

Everything here is fastidiously marshalled to enhance the natural peace and beauty. Sensitively coloured green litterbins are positioned round the island, and even the beach cafés are spotless, with the sand under their benches manicured daily. A law forbids playing radio in the open.

The island jail

Perhaps it's no accident that the person who devoted a lifetime to realising this carefully created paradise was a retired army major. Peter Wood arrived here in 1949 and as the island's tenant owned the hotel, pub, shops, cattle – everything. He died in 1998, but his successors will continue his legacy until the lease expires in 2050.

With very limited hotel, cottage, and camping accommodation, a day trip is the only option for the perhaps thousand visitors who come daily in season, but thankfully the tiny island has enough paths and beaches to absorb the crowds.

Arriving at Herm

The lovely boat ride from St Peter Port follows a route studded with rocky hazards and safety beacons. **Herm Harbour** is a wading pool at low tide. If you arrive when the harbour is not receiving, your boat lands a quarter of a mile south at the **Rosière Steps**. Either way, just follow the path to the 'village',

Rosière Steps

which in reality is home to the island's only hotel, pub and restaurant *(see pages 135 and 142)* and, in a central *piazza* (built by Italian workers in 1963), three gift shops in pastel-painted cottages.

In the hotel grounds there is a windowless **jail** barely big enough for one prisoner, built of granite in 1826. Claims are often made that it is the smallest jail in the world. The gift shops sell a selection of beach gear, Guernsey sweaters and countless other souvenirs that provide proof that you have actually visited the island, including: Herm scissors, Herm rubbers, Herm drinks coasters, Herm mustard, Herm teddies, and the much-prized Herm stamps. The island issued its own stamps between 1953 and 1969, used on up to 200,000 items of mail annually.

Around the Island

Neat turquoise signs say how many minutes it should take to reach destinations down the sandy paths which lead to the beaches and cliffs, or how long it will take to criss-cross the interior. You could make it right round the 500 acres (200 hectares) in less than two hours, or happily spend an entire week exploring them. All over the island, Herm's 110

Herm oysters

Herm's famous oyster beds are on the west coast of the island around Fisherman's Beach. They are usually on the menu at the restaurant of the White House Hotel.

Guernsey cows – one of the bailiwick's largest herds – graze in fields above the sea.

To the north, the footpath winds between the honey-suckle and the sea. **Fisherman's Beach** is muddy and rocky beyond the sand at low tide, so is generally uncrowded. Beyond that, the path skirts a two-person **cemetery**, not much bigger than a king-sized bed. It's a reminder of a cholera epidemic of 1832; the victims were travellers on a passing ship.

Here the path forks; the inland route cuts across the grass and dunes of **The Common**, a popular haunt of rabbits, surrounded by prickly burnet roses, sea holly and thyme. At **Robert's Cross** you can see what remains of a prehistoric tomb, a Neolithic passage grave 16ft (4.8m) long. A crude obelisk north of here marks where a large prehistoric menhir stood; it was exported by quarrymen in the 19th century as just another hunk of granite.

The northeast coast of the island is occupied by the dazzling, long expanse of **Shell Beach**. Through a quirk of the tides, strips of shells from perhaps thousands of miles away gravitate here – along with the many sunbathers and swimmers. Conchologists go wild over Warty Venus, Hunchback Scallops, Dwarf Winkles and Painted Tops, while amateurs suddenly turn into collectors. The beach café sells a guide to the 50 most interesting shells. Sunbathers, especially children, should be coated liberally with sunscreen as Shell Beach has the highest incidence of sunburn in the Channel Islands.

Continuing clockwise is a popular small, sandy, sheltered beach, **Belvoir Bay**. Inland up a steep, shaded path is **Le Manoir**, the *real* village where the islanders live. Here there is an unobtrusive power station, a workshop, cottages, primary school, and the tenant's home. What appears to be a medieval keep was actually built within the past century by an earlier tenant, Prince Blücher. A genuine medieval building is the 11th-century **chapel** dedicated to the obscure Saint Tugual. Its garden has a pretty, pint-sized bell tower.

Looking east and south, Herm's **cliffs** can't compete in height with those of the bigger islands, but they're ruggedly overgrown with bramble, unfrequented, and populated with campion, sea pinks, and samphire. A path leads past **Barbara's Leap**, from where a young woman fell and survived. From the southern extremity at **Point Sauzebourge**, you look onto the flat-topped private island of **Jethou**. Its 1920s owner, the writer Sir Compton Mackenzie, called it 'the most perfect small island off the coast of Britain'. Puffins nest on Jethou's couple of offshore islands.

Shell Beach, where the sun burns brightest

WHAT TO DO

SPORTS

Jersey and Guernsey cater to all sports lovers, both on the sea and ashore. There are also two leisure centres – one in Fort Regent in St Helier and the other in St Peter Port – where you can work up a sweat on a squash court and cool down in a large indoor pool. Unsurprisingly, there is far less in the way of organised activity on the smaller islands.

Watersports

Swimming. At the beach, keep in mind the tides, which rise with startling speed, as well as the potential danger of submerged rocks. A few beaches have lifeguards, but generally safety must be your own concern.

Scuba diving. Qualified divers on all the islands can go out with local clubs in expeditions to fish-thronged cliffs, rocks and caves, or sunken war relics. As the currents are always tricky, advice and assistance are essential. On Jersey, the Bowley Bay Diving Centre (tel: 01534-866990; www.scuba divingjersey.com) offers tuition, as do Dive Guernsey (tel: 01481-714525; www.diveguernsey.co.uk) and School of Diving/Sarnia SkinDivers (tel: 01481-722884) on Guernsey.

Surfing. The most renowned venue is St Ouen's Bay, Jersey, where the rollers are up to championship standard. Participants' efforts make for an exciting spectator sport, or you can join in by hiring boards, wetsuits and professional instructors. Guernsey's top surfing beach is Vazon Bay, but the waves aren't as impressive or reliable as on Jersey, and there are no facilities for unequipped visitors.

Opportunities for fishing abound in the Channel Islands

Windsurfing. A steady breeze blows on the coastlines of Jersey and Guernsey, making these two islands ideal for windsurfing. You'll find boards for hire and qualified instructors on hand at St Brelade's, St Aubin's and Grouville bays on Jersey, and Cobo, Ladies and L'Ancresse bays on Guernsey.

Sailing. Thousands of yachts visit the islands' marinas each year. Experienced sailors can, if they so wish, charter unskippered yachts and sail to other islands or France, or discover hidden coves closer to home. Of the islands, Jersey is best organised for hiring boats. Contact the St Helier Yacht Club (tel: 01534-721307; www.shyc.je), Tarka Sea Trips (tel: 01534-858046) or St Brelade's Windsurfing and Sailing School (tel: 07797-717564); on Guernsey contact the Guernsey Yacht Club (tel: 01481-722838; www.gyc.org.uk).

Other watersports. If all you want is to potter about on the water in a canoe, rowing boat or pedalo, St Brelade's Bay on Jersey has the most on offer. On both Jersey and Guernsey the more daring water-babies can waterski, jetski, parascend or even ride on a towed inflatable banana. For a selection of these activities on Jersey, try St Brelade's Bay, La Haule in St Aubin's Bay or the Gorey end of the Royal Bay of Grouville; on Guernsey visit L'Ancresse Bay.

Fishing. Because of the Channel's mighty tides, an exceptional variety of species can be hooked. The Guernsey Tourist Office (see page 124) sells an excellent angling booklet covering tackle dealers, boats to charter and the best places to fish and even collect bait. Jersey's tourist office (see page 124) provides some advice; a fishing boat can be chartered on Alderney.

Alderney cricket

Alderney Island has a well-appointed cricket ground, Les Butes, with wonderful sea views. John Arlott, the late BBC commentator, lived on the island and was chairman of the club. Ian Botham once had a house here, too.

Acres of sand for playing at Plémont Bay

Sports Ashore

Cycling. There are bike hire shops in the major centres. Guernsey has a network of lanes suitable for cycling, called Ruettes Tranquilles, while on Sark, where cars are banned, bikes are a popular way of getting around *(see page 109)*. Unlike Sark, Herm does not allow cycling.

Golf. The addition of new, expanded courses has angered conservationists, but lightened the pressure on the islands' oversubscribed existing links. Top players compete in the Jersey Open in June at La Moye (tel: 01534-747166). Here and at the Royal Jersey (tel: 01534-854416) you need proof of handicap to play, while Les Mielles (tel: 01534-482787), the Jersey Recreation Ground (9 holes; tel: 01534-721938), Wheatlands (9 holes; tel: 01534-888844) and Les Ormes (9 holes; tel: 01534-497000) welcome all players. On Guernsey, for the 18-hole Royal Guernsey seaside course by L'Ancresse Bay (tel: 01481-245070) you need to be a club member, but the new La Grande Mare (18 holes on 14 greens; tel: 01481-256576) and the 9-hole course of the St Pierre Park Hotel (tel: 01481-728282) welcome all. Alderney has a terrific, under-used 9-hole course open to all (tel: 01481-822835).

Horse riding and racing. On the sand, along tree-lined paths or across open fields, riding is always scenic on the isles of Jersey and Guernsey. Schools have instructors, horses and ponies: tourist offices have the details *(see pages 124–5)*. Jersey revives old-time horse-racing at Les Landes, above the sea.

Motor racing. St Ouen's Bay, Jersey, hosts motorcycle and car races. In Guernsey, similar excitement centres on the vast stretch of Vazon Bay; there are hill climbs on Val des Terres and beach racing at Ladies Bay.

In Search of Peace

To escape from it all, head either for Jersey's north coast or the south coast of Guernsey, where company comes in the form of screeching seagulls, rustling bracken and intoxicatingly scented hedgerows.

The views are stupendous – of sheer rockfaces topped by a coating of green plunging into a navy-blue sea. On Jersey you can walk the 15 miles (24km) of well-marked cliff paths all the way from Grosnez Castle east to Rozel and a similar length on Guernsey from La Valette, south of St Peter Port, west to Pleinmont Point. Frequent sandy coves, cafés and pubs provide happy distraction on the way. Armed with a local bus timetable *(see page 126)*, you can work out when and where to be picked up and need not retrace your steps.

Should the terrain prove too strenuous, look for 'Green Lanes' that traverse the interiors of both islands. If you demand more action, then a stroll on Herm, a trek along the remote south coast of Alderney and rambles round the walking heaven of Sark await. Bookshops *(see page 94)*, tourist offices *(see pages 124–5)* and, on Jersey, the North Coast Visitor Centre at Grève de Lecq provide detailed walking guides.

Sand yachting at St Ouen's Bay

Tennis. The Jersey Recreation Grounds (tel: 01534-721938), Caesarean Tennis Club (tel: 01534-789321) and Les Ormes (indoor courts; tel: 01534-497000); Guernsey's Beau Séjour Leisure Centre (tel: 01481-747210; www.freedomzone.gg) and Guernsey Tennis Centre, St Sampson's (tel: 01481-712182); and the Alderney Tennis Club (tel: 01481-823295) have plenty of courts.

SHOPPING

The Channel Islands are the next best thing to a duty-free zone. Duties are low and Value Added Tax (VAT) nonexistent. Shops displaying a Fair Trader sign promise to pass on tax benefits. The best bargains are luxury items such as jewellery and perfume, but some customs restrictions apply *(see page 113)*. As well as browsing shops and department stores in and around King Street, St Helier and St Peter Port's High

Street, you should also try to make for the town's indoor markets to ogle the daily catch and the flower stalls, and head out to the islands' craft workshops. On Thursday afternoons in summer there are craft stalls in Market Street in St Peter Port manned by people in period costume.

What To Look For

Alcohol. The low prices are the chief attraction. Consider liqueurs produced using the rich local cream or Jersey's native wine from La Mare Wine Estate *(see page 42)*, which has a shop selling its produce, Maison la Mare in King Street, St Helier. On Guernsey, fine wine specialist award-winners Sommelier Wine (23 St George Esplanade, St Peter Port; tel: 01481-721677) has a huge range.

Antiques. Expensive antiques and cheaper bric-à-brac can be found on the cobbled Mill and Mansell streets in St Peter Port.

Books. From guides to local flora and fauna to personal accounts on life under the German occupation, hundreds of books have been written about the islands. Waterstone's in Queen Street and The Printed Word at the Jersey Museum, St Helier; and Guernsey Press in Smith Street and The Bookshop, The Bridge, St Peter Port, have good selections.

Shopping in St Peter Port

Ceramics. You can watch craftspeople turn out hand-finished items in the islands' potteries. Jersey Pottery *(see page 47)* sells expensive pots and crockery. On Guernsey, the Moulin Huet Pottery and Craft Centre at St Martin display one-off pieces.

Flowers. Freesias, carnations, roses and other island grown

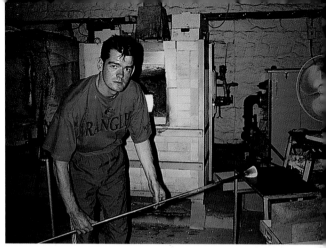

Glass blowing at Guernsey's Oatlands Village

flowers are inexpensive to carry home, if home is in Britain. Visit the Sunset Nurseries, St Peter, where you can buy fresh-cut flowers or have them dispatched to the UK. On Guernsey there's the Guernsey Freesia Centre, Route Carre (close to Oatlands, tel: 01481-248185).

Jewellery. From self-service emporia to smarter outlets, the number of jewellers in St Helier and St Peter Port is quite simply overwhelming. They sell everything from miniature silver milk cans to gold chain by the yard. Devotees should also visit Jersey Goldsmiths *(see pages 35–6)* and Jersey Pearl *(see page 40)* and Guernsey's Bruce Russell & Son, Le Gron, St Saviour's, and Catherine Best (Old Mill, St Martin's).

Knitwear. Although most are commercially produced today, the familiar fishermen's sweaters *(see page 58)* carry on a proud tradition. Jersey sweaters are made and sold at Jersey Woollen Mills, Five Mile Road, St Ouen; for Guernseys visit the factory shop of Le Tricoteur at Perelle on the west coast.

Perfumes. Chic brands are sold at seductive prices from the towns' many fragrant stores. Some sell island-made scents based on local wild flowers, as does the Jersey Lavender Farm *(see page 37)*, while Samarès Manor *(see pages 48–9)* makes and sells sweet-smelling lily and sandalwood soaps.

Stamps *(see pages 30, 71 and 85)*. Philatelists are drawn to the main post offices in Jersey and Guernsey, where definitive and commemorative sets and first-day covers for the respective bailiwicks and Alderney are all sold. Sub-post offices on Alderney, Sark and Herm also appeal to collectors.

Other crafts. The islands of Jersey and Guernsey have candle workshops at Plémont and St Sampson, where you can watch wax being dyed and moulded, and purchase the final products. Guernsey Woodcarvers offers appealing decorative artefacts such as ducks and fruit. For a really unusual souvenir, how about one of Jersey Woodturner's walking sticks made from stalks of Jersey's famous giant cabbages? *(see page 49)*. Guernsey's Oatlands Village *(see page 66)* provides a convenient one-stop shop for all sorts of hand-made items, from beeswax candles to perfume bottles. At the Strawberry Farm (St Saviour) there is a pottery and visitors can also see how the traditional Guernsey is knitted.

Jersey Lavender Farm

ENTERTAINMENT

The Channel Islands follow a simple rule: the bigger the island, the livelier and more varied the nightlife.

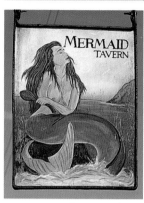

Jersey offers something for all generations. There is live music at The Bridge (Weighbridge), Chambers, Blue Note or Fort Regent. For nightclubs in St Helier try Folies (The Esplanade), Liquid (The Waterfront) or Pure (Caledonia Place).

Enticing pub sign

Cabaret and dance shows are often hosted by hotels (see the *Jersey Evening Post*). Pubs often feature live jazz, folk and amateur nights. The revamped Opera House (tel: 01534-511115; www.jerseyoperahouse.co. uk) and the multi-faceted Jersey Arts Centre (tel: 01534-700444/400) lay on theatre, dance, classical and jazz concerts. St Helier has two cinemas: The Forum in Bath Street (tel: 01534-871611; www.forum.je) and Cineworld UK, the Waterfront (tel: 0871-200 2000; www.cineworld.co.uk).

Guernsey has fewer nightclubs but as many music pubs as Jersey. Nightclubs include Club 54 and Folies, North Plantation. There is live music most nights at the Doghouse (tel: 01481-721302; www.doghouse.gg) and Blind O'Reilly's, The Bridge (tel: 01481-244503). See the *Guernsey Press* for details of gigs and for music at St James's Concert Hall (tel: 01481-711360; www.stjames.gg). Theatre is on at Guernsey's Beau Séjour Leisure Centre (tel: 01481-747210; www.freedomzone.gg). For film there is the Mallard (tel: 01481-266366) and CinéGuernsey (tel: 01481-726518).

CHILDREN'S CHANNEL ISLANDS

The Channel Islands are a great place to take the kids on holiday. Importantly, the islands feel very safe. Jersey and Guernsey provide acres of sandy **beaches** for making sandcastles and for ball games, and many of them are gently sloping with safe bathing. Jersey has the most to do if the weather's not great.

Jersey Zoo provides a fail-safe half-day of entertainment and education, while **Living Legend**'s high-tech extravaganza will excite any youngster with imagination. The hands-on exhibits at the Maritime Museum, farmyard animals at Hamptonne, and parrot and falconry shows at Samarès Manor will all appeal to youngsters.

Guernsey, like Jersey, has a good leisure centre, a castle to explore and World War II museums that should appeal to most ages. Sausmarez Manor in St Martin has two 'adventure play areas' and a 9-hole 'pitch and putt' golf attraction. Oatland Village's facilities also include children's rides.

There aren't quite so many attractions on the smaller islands, so children – and parents – need to be more creative in keeping occupied. They may, however, fall in love with the islands' quaint ways. Because of the considerable walking and cycling involved and because of the inaccessibility of its beaches, **Sark** can be tough-going for young children. **Herm**, by contrast, where Shell Beach is just a 10-minute walk from the ferry, is paradise for any short-legged adventurer.

Children's ride at Oatlands Craft Centre, Guernsey

Calendar of Events

The tourist boards have precise dates of events, which can change from year to year. See also www.jerseytravel.com, www.visitguernsey.com, www.alderney.gov.gg and www.sark-tourism.com.

May. *International Arts Festival* (Jersey): A week of musical events by international performers, art exhibitions, talks and workshops. *Guernsey Ale and Food Festival*: Two weeks of local ales and classic pub grub. *Milk-a-Punch Sunday* (Alderney): Every island publican serves milk, egg and rum cocktails. *Liberation Day* (9 May, Jersey and Guernsey): Commemorative celebrations. *Foire de Jersey*: Traditional country fayre. *Alderney Wildlife Festival Week*: Events organised by Alderney Wildlife Trust.

June. *Jersey Festival of Motoring*: Five days of events and displays for the motoring enthusiast. *Midsummer Jersey*: Folklore, food fairs and al fresco music and film. *Midsummer Show* (Sark): Showcase for Sark's gardeners.

July. *Jersey Garden Festival*: A week of nature walks, flower-arranging and open gardens. *Sheep Race Meeting* (Sark): Sheep and their teddy jockeys race over a set course. *Jazz in The Park* (Jersey): A one-day 'ultimate picnic opportunity' in Howard Park. *Viaer Marchi* (Guernsey): Re-enactment of a traditional open-air market in Saumarez Park. *Town Carnival* (Guernsey): Music and street events in St Peter Port. *The Jersey Festival of Football*: Five-a-side community youth football.

August. *Hamptonne Fair* (Jersey): Three-day hands-on craft fair. *Battle of Flowers* (Jersey and Guernsey): A highlight of Jersey's year – a parade of flower-festooned floats, with musicians, dancers and entertainers; on Guernsey it is the climax to the *North Show* country fair. *Alderney Week*: the island's big carnival event with all sorts of competitions. *Sark Carnival*: Sark's most popular annual charity event with stalls and games. *Vale Earth Fair* (Guernsey): One-day (and night) music festival held at Vale Castle in aid of humanitarian causes; music, dance tent, bar, food, stalls and children's area.

September. *Jersey Regatta*: The flagship sailing event. *Grand Autumn Show* (Sark): Two-day agricultural show. In *Battle of Britain Week* both main islands enjoy a free air display. *Victor Hugo International Music Festival* (Guernsey): Week-long biennial event of international classical and folk music.

EATING OUT

Whether you lean toward sophisticated gourmet food or homespun cooking, you'll eat well in the Channel Islands. Annual culinary competitions testify to the islands' gastronomic pride. Many restaurants, used to a well-off, discerning clientele, aspire to haute cuisine, while ploughman's lunches, pizzas and cream teas satisfy the less demanding.

Where to Eat

You're rarely far from food in the Channel Islands. Almost every attraction and easily accessible beach has at least a café, an ancient inn lurks down most country lanes, and hotels invariably woo non-residents with cream teas, bar meals and gourmet menus.

Your choice of venue may depend as much on the kind of place that you want to eat in – a snug pub, a rambling farmhouse, a smart restaurant or simply a spot with grand views of a harbour or beach.

The islands' million annual visitors are catered for in some 400 hotels and guesthouses and 300 restaurants. Much of the food is mass produced for tourists, and the main centres

Food Festivals

In order to promote an image of gourmet living, and to boost low-season tourism, the islands hold regular food festivals and 'Taste of' events throughout the year. International cuisine is also given a boost through festivals of French, Norman, Spanish, Portuguese and even Irish food. Jersey and Guernsey hold an annual 'Tennerfest' in the autumn, during which meals at some 40 restaurants can be had for just £10.

ensure there is provision for the standard fish-and-chips, pizzas, burgers and crepes. Brasseries and seafood restaurants may offer some of the best local food, but there is also good fresh food generally available in pubs and restaurants. In the islands' main towns, cosy *trattorie* predominate (particularly on Halkett Place in St Helier and Le Pollet in St Peter Port), while a smattering of French, Portuguese, Chinese and Indian establishments provide other cosmopolitan touches. Some of the better restaurants are to be found in hotels, such as the Victor Hugo in the St Pierre Park Hotel in

Home-grown menu

St Peter Port, and some offer special 'gourmet breaks' with five-course meals to end your bracing day of walking along the shores.

Choice is clearly more limited on the small islands, but there is no reason why you should not eat well there too, with the hotels again providing some of the better choices. Some of the restaurant proprietors are also fishermen, so go for the catch of the day.

The islands have gourmet aspirations and outside the run-of-the-mill establishments – and outside of the high season – discerning, well-off residents ensure there are excellent meals to be had. Competitions are regularly organised among the restaurants and the results are well publicised.

Crabs and lobsters are island specialities

For self-caterers, there are plenty of places to find fresh food, from St Helier's grand Central Market to humble farms and fish stalls.

What to Eat

Despite the islands' proximity to France, traditional British cooking has the upper hand. You can start off with a fry-up, have roast beef with Yorkshire pudding for lunch (the British institution of Sunday lunch is well-preserved), wade through a full tea of cucumber sandwiches, scones and cakes, and end the day on a sea wall munching greasy fish and chips.

While a Gallic flair is often apparent in fish dishes, French is the language of many menus, which in fact describe British – and sometimes even Italian – cooking. If you're prepared to pay, however, there are plenty of authentic French restaurants, while fresh croissants and baguettes fill many bakery windows.

Seafood has top billing in the islands. Your best bet is the fresh catch often listed on the blackboard outside a restaurant – mussels, scallops, shrimps, spider crabs or lobster (served cold with mayonnaise; 'thermidor', braised in sherry or brandy and served in a mustard-flavoured sauce; or *à la nage*, in a white wine stock), or you could opt for sea bass, sole or brill. Oysters, which used to thrive along the coasts, are now successfully farmed. Unless you choose a café's crab sandwich, seafood can be pricey. Fish is often served by weight – ask roughly how much a dish will cost to avoid an unpleasant surprise at the end of the meal.

As for the islands' **agricultural produce**, Jersey new potatoes – Jersey Royals – are delicious, preferably garnished with butter and parsley, or mint. Other Channel Islands vegetables win much praise: succulent Guernsey tomatoes, familiarly known as 'Guernsey Toms', mass-produced under glass; cauliflowers; celery; and courgettes.

A number of **native delicacies** remain. Though cafés at a few attractions still serve some of them, most are becoming increasingly difficult to find. The **ormer**, a large mollusc related to the abalone found in the northern Pacific, Australia, South Africa – and nowhere north of the islands – is now rare as a result of overfishing. They are almost as painstaking to prepare as **black butter**, which, despite its name, is a dairy-free concoction made from apples, sugar, lemons, liquorice and cider. The preserve was made in large quantities in the 19th century when the islands had thriving cider industries. It takes 24 hours of non-stop work to create the brew.

Island lobsters

In the late 19th century around 4,000 lobsters were caught off the islands every week, mostly for restaurants abroad, and until recent times Belgian restaurateurs would fly in to snap up the day's catch to take back for their evening menu.

Other venerable recipes include the bean jar or crock, containing several kinds of beans, plus some pork, onions and herbs (Jersey emigrants in Canada are reputed to have inspired Mr Heinz's now world-famous baked beans), as well as conger-eel soup, enhanced with marigold petals.

Local **pastry** is easy to find throughout the islands. The Jersey Wonders traditionally cooked as the tide went out, are a variation on the doughnut, twisted into a neat figure of eight. *Fiottes* are balls of sweet pastry poached in milk, usually eaten at Easter, and the ubiquitous Guernsey *gâche* (pronounced gosh) is a tasty fruitcake.

Dairy Products

The Channel Islands are famous for their herds of Jersey and Guernsey cows producing incomparably rich milk, the source of butter the colour of wild buttercups and cream

Going along with the herd

often lavished on scones, strawberries and desserts. Products include crème fraiches and yoghurts as well as clotted cream. Jersey makes Wickedly Tempting ice cream and Guernsey has a variety of cheddar-style cheeses.

Drinks

St Helier's home brew

The islanders' favourite drink from Norman to relatively recent times was **cider**. The La Mare Wine Estate *(see page 42)* is also a cider maker, producing a bottle-conditioned cider called *pomette*. It also produced **Jersey Apple Brandy**, which is double distilled in 100-year-old oak casks. Cider Festivals (La Fais'sie d'Cidre) are held in the autumn.

Today the preferred tipple is a pint of **beer**, as in the United Kingdom, though not all pubs sell real ale. There are two local breweries. Jersey Brewer in Longueville, St Saviour, produces a 'hoppy' Jersey Best and a sweeter Jersey Special. The Tipsy Toad brewery in St Helier has its own pub, the Star, converted from a former warehouse. Their range of beers includes a seasonal Festival Toad, at a full strength 8 percent.

Oenophiles can also take advantage of the relatively low price of restaurant **wines**. Jersey's single vineyard produces several wines, including a dry oak-fermented white, sparkling wines (white Cuvée de la Mare and pink Lille) and a red called Bailiwick, which is made from Pinot Noire grapes.

HANDY TRAVEL TIPS

An A–Z Summary of Practical Information

A

ACCOMMODATION (See also CAMPING and RECOMMENDED HOTELS)

Jersey and Guernsey. From simple bed and breakfasts to top-of-the-range country-house hotels, both islands offer accommodation to meet almost every budget and taste. While much is of the kind you find in old-fashioned British seaside resorts – small guesthouses serving high tea at 6.30pm, for example – many of the most attractive hotels are converted from old farmhouses. The islands are so small that even if you stay inland you'll still be within a few minutes' drive of the beaches. For a traditional beach hotel, head for St Brelade's Bay on Jersey or the west coast of Guernsey: St Peter Port is a good place to base yourself here.

Accommodation is rigorously inspected and graded on both islands. For their facilities and quality, Jersey hotels are awarded from one to five 'suns' and guesthouses one to three 'diamonds'. In Guernsey, hotels are graded one to five 'crowns' and guesthouses 'D' to 'A'. Much of the accommodation is mediocre; the recommended hotels section *(see page 128)* will help you find an appealing place to stay.

Both tourist boards produce excellent brochures detailing prices and facilities for all the islands' registered accommodation. Details of accommodation on Alderney, Sark and Herm are included in Guernsey's accommodation brochure. The islands' tourist offices can provide help with availability *(see pages 124–5)*: telephone 01534-500888 for Jersey and 01481-723555 for Guernsey. Help is also available at the airports and ports.

Alderney. The island has several modest hotels and about a dozen guesthouses. Many offer terms including Aurigny flights and taxi transfer to and from the airport.

Sark. The island's five hotels include some of the most seductive of any in the Channel Islands. All encourage half-board arrangements.

For those on a budget there are a dozen guesthouses.
Herm. For Herm's only hotel, *see page 135.*

Self Catering

Much of the self-catering on **Jersey** is in units affiliated to hotels and guesthouses. The tourist board has a list of these and some independent self-catering establishments; also try the Jersey-based tour operator Freedom Holidays (tel: 01534-725259; www.free domholidays.com). **Guernsey** inspects and grades self-catering from 'C' to 'A' and provides comprehensive details, including prices and facilities in their general accommodation brochure. **Alderney** and **Sark** offer self-catering too: contact their tourist offices. For utter isolation, Fort Clonque *(see page 134)* on **Alderney** sleeps up to 13 and can be rented from the Landmark Trust (tel: 01628-825925). For a list of self-catering accommodation see www.visitalderney.com. **Herm** offers 20 extremely popular, characterful cottages and flats (tel: 01481-722377; www.herm-island. com/selfcatering).

There is one **youth hostel** on the Channel Islands: YHA Jersey, Haut de la Garenne, La Rue de la Pouclee des Quatre; tel: 01534-840100; www.yha.org.uk. It has rooms with 2, 4, 5, 6 and 6+ beds.

AIRPORTS

Jersey and **Guernsey** airports are microcosms of island life. Offshore stockbrokers and businesspeople mingle with tourists and children straight off the beach. Though busy, they are distinctly unstressful places compared to big international airports. The walk to and from the plane is short, as is the wait for your luggage. Both have food outlets, tourist information desks and bureau de change facilities. Prices for spirits, cigarettes and perfumes are comparable to those found in the towns, while shops also sell locally grown fresh flowers. Rental cars can be picked up from the terminals, as can buses and taxis. For Jersey Airport information, tel: 01534-446000, www2.jerseyairport.com; for Guernsey Airport, tel: 01481-237766, www.guernsey-airport.gov.gg.

Alderney Airport is a wonderful little place. The terminal looks remarkably like a ramshackle cricket pavilion, while two of the three runways are grass. Aurigny and Blue Islands fly here. Taxis meet arriving planes and rental cars can be booked.

B

BICYCLE HIRE

Jersey and **Guernsey** are small and flat enough to make cycling pleasant; **Alderney's** size and its peaceful lanes are ideal for cyclists. On motor-free **Sark**, pedal power is the preferred means of transport, and you should keep to the left despite the absence of cars. It's hard to miss the bicycle hire shops on Sark; in high season, book a bike in advance through Isle of Sark Shipping *(see page 125)*. On Jersey, Guernsey and Alderney the tourist boards publish lists of bicycle hire shops – some also hire out mountain bikes, tandems and mopeds; for the latter you need a driving licence.

BUDGETING FOR YOUR TRIP

Here are some guideline prices. Please note that prices vary greatly from one establishment to the next and that inflation takes its toll.

Accommodation. High season prices for a double room: B&B £40–£70; mid-range hotel £60–£120; luxury hotel £120–£200.

Airport transfer. Taxi to St Helier £12; to St Peter Port £11.

Bicycle hire. £7 a day, £30 a week. £6 a day on Sark.

Buses. Jersey: single fares 90p–£1.60; 1-day pass £6, 3 days £15.30, 5 days £22.50. Guernsey: one trip costs 50p any distance, much less with Wave & Save smart card.

Car hire. For an economy car, from £32 a day, £132 a week in high season, all inclusive.

Entertainment. Cinema £3.80–£6. Nightclub from £6.

Inter-island travel. (Round-trip prices.) Aurigny flights from £35 one way, £60 return. Ferries: between Jersey and Guernsey, from £20 per person; Guernsey–Sark £18.50; Guernsey–Herm £6.50.

Meals and drinks. Café/pub lunch from £6; restaurant lunch from £12; moderate dinner £20; three-course dinner with drinks, £40; pint of beer from £2.30; bottle of wine from £8.

Petrol. Fuel prices are similar to those in the UK and the EU.

Photography. Colour 35mm film (24 exposures) £4.

Spirits. Litre of whisky £16.

Sports. Round of golf £18–£50. 1-hour horse ride £22. Tennis £7 an hour. Pedalo or canoe £4 for half an hour. Waterski and water-boarding £18. Surfing £30 an hour, £45 a day, £155 for a 5-day course. Windsurfing £15 for an hour course; hire of equipment from £20. Diving £320 basic open-water course.

Taxis. £4.55 for the first mile, £6 after 10pm.

Tours. Jersey day-long coach tour £14.50; Guernsey half-day coach tour £8. Sark 2-hour carriage tour £5 per person.

Trips to France. Jersey/Guernsey–St Malo day round trip from £28.

C

CAMPING

Except on Jersey, where visiting caravans and motorhomes are al-lowed subject to a permit, it's forbidden to import caravans or to pitch a tent anywhere except in a designated site. (You can hire tents as well as bring your own.) On **Jersey**, campsites include: Rose Farm (tel: 01534-741231; www.jerseycamping.com) near St Bre-lade's Bay, which has good facilities including a large heated pool and ready-erected tents; and Rozel Camping Park (tel: 01534-855200; www.jerseyisland.com/country), which also has a pool but is a smaller, more peaceful site in the island's northeast corner.

Guernsey has three attractive sites: Fauxquets Valley Farm Camp-ing Site (tel: 01481-255460; www.fauxquets.co.uk); La Bailloterie

Camping (tel: 01481-243636; www.campinginguernsey.com), in the northeast corner; and Vaugrat Camping (tel: 01481-257468), a short walk from the northwest beaches. **Alderney's** Saye Bay site (tel: 01481-822556; www.visitalderney.com) lies directly behind the north coast's sandy bays. Of **Sark's** two basic sites, La Valette (tel: 01481-832202; www.sark.info) is dramatically situated near the cliffs. **Herm**, too, has a simple, well-run campsite (tel: 01481-722377; www.herm-island.com). Their tourist offices can provide details.

CAR HIRE (See also DRIVING)

Car hire is much cheaper than in the UK and almost anywhere else in Europe. There's usually little difference in the international and local car rental firms' rates in Jersey and Guernsey. The rates quoted include unlimited mileage and insurance. There are cars to hire from the airports and ports; telephone the airports or tourist offices for contacts *(see pages 108–9 and 124–5)*. Car hire is equally cheap on Alderney. There, Alderney Car Hire (tel: 01481-823352) or Braye Hire Cars (tel: 01481-823881) can have a car waiting for you at the airport.

To hire a car, you must be over 21 years of age, and have a driving licence and at least one year's driving experience. Elderly drivers (anything upwards of 70 years old) may have to take out extra insurance through the car-hire company.

Local drivers give a wide berth to hired cars, which are instantly recognisable by their number plate, branded with a big letter 'H'. If you're bringing your own car, you must carry your driving licence and insurance certificate, and display a nationality plate on the back of the vehicle.

CLIMATE AND CLOTHING

The Channel Islands are the sunniest places in the British Isles. Jersey enjoys almost 2,000 hours of sunshine a year. Their southerly, maritime position also ensures mild winters, summers tempered by sea breezes and very variable weather – expect a concoction of fine skies, clouds and rain at any time of year. The sun's rays can be deceptively strong; take the necessary precautions to avoid overexposure. The sea is usually chilly until well into high summer.

Hotels often display weather forecasts in the lobby; consult the local newspapers too *(see page 120)*.

The following chart gives the average maximum temperature for St Helier, Jersey:

	J	F	M	A	M	J	J	A	S	O	N	D
°C	9	8	11	13	16	19	21	21	19	16	12	10
°F	48	46	52	55	61	66	70	70	66	61	54	50

Clothing. Even in mid-summer, take a sweater and waterproofs. However, a T-shirt, shorts and a bathing costume should suffice on most summer days. All the islands have enticing coast and country paths, so bring appropriate walking footwear. As for formality: topless bathing is not encouraged on the beaches; swimwear is inappropriate in the towns; nightclubs and discos usually ban trainers; in better restaurants men are expected to wear smart casual for dinner.

COMPLAINTS

If you have a serious complaint to make about a business and the manager or your tour-operator representative cannot resolve the matter to your satisfaction, contact the Jersey or Guernsey tourist boards, preferably before you return home. Both tourist boards have complaints forms to fill in.

CRIME AND SAFETY (see also EMERGENCIES and POLICE)

Don't be misled by the BBC detective series *Bergerac*: the Channel Islands are relatively very safe places to take a holiday. The local papers rarely report anything more serious than a drunken brawl or shoplifting (except maybe for the occasional drugs haul). On the smaller islands, many front doors are left permanently off the latch. Nonetheless, particularly on Jersey and Guernsey, don't leave valuables unattended or cars unlocked. The Channel Islands take a very serious attitude to drugs; in Guernsey fines for small amounts of cannabis begin at £400; for Class A drugs imprisonment is likely.

CUSTOMS AND ENTRY REQUIREMENTS

A passport is not required for travel within the Common Travel Area (United Kingdom, Republic of Ireland, Channel Islands and the Isle of Man), although the majority of airlines do require that you produce photo ID at check-in. Passengers arriving from outside of this Common Travel Area will pass through an Immigration control, for which the Channel Islands have the same passport and visa requirements as the UK. Citizens from Australia, Canada, New Zealand, South Africa and the United States need valid passports but no visa. A passport is needed for trips to France.

Duty-free allowance. Customs allowances are not as relaxed as elsewhere in the EU, as the Channel Islands is not a full member. Each adult arriving from the EU (including the UK) is permitted the following duty-free levels for alcohol and cigarettes: 200 cigarettes or 50 cigars or 250g tobacco; 2 litres still table wine and 1 litre of spirits or 2 litres of fortified/sparkling wine or 2 additional litres of still table wine; 60cc/ml perfume; 250cc/ml toilet water; £145 worth of other gifts (watches, jewellery, cameras, etc).

Restrictions if entering from outside the EU are as follows:

	Cigarettes		Cigars		Tobacco	Wine	Beer	Spirits
Ireland:	200	or	50	or	250g	2l	or	1l
Australia:	250		or		250g	1l alcohol		
Canada:	200	&	50	&	1kg	1.1l or 8.5l or 1.1l		
New Zealand:	200	or	50	or	250g	4.5l or 4.5l & 1.1l		
South Africa:	400	&	50	&	250g	2l	&	1l
US:	200	or	50	or	2kg	1l alcohol		

D

DRIVING

Jersey and Guernsey are relatively small, so it is possible to explore them without a car. Both also have good bus systems *(see page 126)*. Walking or cycling may be preferable, especially on Alderney.

Driving conditions. It's claimed that **Jersey** has the highest ratio of cars to people of anywhere in Europe. The island's populous parts often suffer the kind of traffic problems you were hoping to forget, with lengthy queues and problems with parking. Fortunately, the traffic spreads out over more than 500 miles (800km) of road and tranquillity may be found only a few minutes from the capital. **Guernsey's** traffic problems are also acute. Furthermore, islanders seem perversely proud of how easy it is to get lost within the maze of lanes: roads are not numbered and often not named and destinations unsigned. Yet the island is so small you know that you'll always hit one major landmark – the sea – pretty soon. Many of Guernsey's lanes are particularly narrow. Convex mirrors help on some blind turnings, but in the main it's simply a question of nosing out very cautiously to see if the coast is clear.

Rules of the road. On all three main islands traffic keeps to the left, despite the efforts of the World War II German occupation forces to change this ancient British tradition. Seat belts must be worn and there are stiff penalties for drinking and driving. A yellow line at a junction means 'Stop'. In **Guernsey** and **Alderney**, a large yellow arrow painted in the road does not mean one-way traffic, but that a yellow 'Stop' line is about 90ft (30m) away. A 'Filter in Turn' sign at a busy intersection means cars must alternate with those coming from other directions. Despite the prevalence of racy sports cars, the Channel Islands are not places to open up the throttle. On **Jersey**, the speed limit is 40mph (65kmh), down to 30mph (50kmh) or 20mph (32kmh) in built-up areas, and 15mph (25kmh) in green lanes. **Guernsey's** speed limit is 35mph (55kmh) and

25mph (40kmh) in built-up areas. **Alderney's** 35mph (55kmh) limit is cut to 20mph (30kmh) in St Anne and comes down further to 12mph (19kmh) on the town's main street.

Parking. On all the islands, a single yellow line (confusingly equivalent to the UK's double yellow line) prohibits parking at any time of the day or night and is strictly enforced. In St Helier park in one of the multi-storey car parks. Pay and display cards are available from car hire companies, garages and shops but *not* in the car parks. Some free parking is controlled by parking discs, provided by car-hire companies, Jersey Tourism or the town hall in St Austin.

Though all parking is free on **Guernsey**, you must use your parking clock (issued by the car-hire company) in car parks and for street parking marked as disc zones. Short-term parking spaces on St Peter Port's quays are usually easy to find, unlike longer-term parking spaces; if you're taking a day trip to one of the islands consider leaving the car at the hotel and getting the bus or taxi to the harbour.

E

ELECTRICITY

The current on the Channel Islands is 240 volts AC. Overseas visitors (UK excepted) should bring an adapter.

EMBASSIES AND CONSULATES

Australia: Australian High Commission, Australia House, The Strand, London WC2B 4LA; tel: (020) 7379-4334; www.australia.org.uk.

Canada: Canadian High Commission, 38 Grosvenor Street, London W1K 4AA; tel: (020) 7258-6600; www.canada.org.uk.

New Zealand: New Zealand High Commission, New Zealand House, 80 Haymarket, London SW1 Y4TQ; tel: (020) 7930-8422; www.nzembassy.com.

Republic of Ireland: Irish Embassy, 17 Grosvenor Place, London SW1X 7HR; tel: (020) 7235-2171. Also Honorary Consul, La Minou, La Rue de la Pigeonnaire, St Brelade, Jersey, JE3 8DE; tel: 01534-745551; www.ireland.embassyhomepage.com.

South Africa: South African High Commission, South Africa House, Trafalgar Square, London WC2N 5DP; tel: (020) 7451-7299; www.southafricahouse.com.

United States: American Citizen Services Unit, US Embassy, 55/56 Upper Brook Street, London, W1A 2LQ; tel: (020) 7499-9000; www.usembassy.org.uk.

EMERGENCIES

The all-purpose number to dial in an emergency (for police, fire, ambulance or sea rescue) is 999.

G

GETTING TO THE CHANNEL ISLANDS

Tourist boards *(see pages 124–5)* provide comprehensive lists of air and ferry services from the UK and other European destinations to the Channel Islands. Your local travel agent should also be able to supply details.

From the UK

By air. Between Easter and autumn, direct flights to Jersey and Guernsey are available from around 20 UK airports. In the off-season the number of flights from regional airports falls considerably. It's definitely worth shopping around for the most competitive fares. Cheaper fares are less flexible, usually with minimum and/or maximum stay restrictions, often including a Saturday night. For the cheapest fares book well in advance, particularly if travelling in July or August. Flybe.com (www.flybe.com) has frequent last-minute offers online. Aurigny flies from London, Bristol,

Manchester and Southampton. Blue Islands flies from Bournemouth and Brighton.

By sea. Condor *(see page 125)* operates a frequent passenger and car-carrying catamaran service to Jersey from Poole (3 hours) or from Weymouth (3½ hours). A similar timetable is operated to Guernsey from Weymouth (2 hours) and from Poole (2½ hours). Condor also operates a traditional 'clipper' service from Portsmouth to Guernsey (7 hours) and on to Jersey (10½ hours) six days a week.

To Alderney, Sark and Herm. For Alderney, Aurigny *(see page 125)* flies from Southampton, and Blue Islands has direct flights from Bournemouth. There are also plane or ferry connections with Guernsey or Jersey *(see pages 125–6)*.

From Abroad

From the US, Canada, Australia, New Zealand and South Africa. The most efficient route is via London Gatwick, from which frequent daily flights serve both Jersey and Guernsey.

From the Republic of Ireland. There are direct flights from Dublin and Cork to Jersey and from Dublin to Guernsey.

Package holidays. Only a few operators have programmes that allow you to stay on more than one island. The islands' tourist boards provide details on the dozens of UK tour operators with Channel Islands programmes. Overseas visitors should contact the British Tourist Authority in their own country (www.visit britain.com).

GUIDED TOURS

Jersey. All-day and half-day coach tours around Jersey cover most island sights and the coast. Tantivy Blue Coach Tours (tel: 01534-706706; www.tantivybluecoach.com). Waverley Coaches (tel: 01534-758360). Minibusdirect (tel: 01534-853287; www.jerseyminibus. com). South Coast Cruises (tel: 01534-732466; www.thisisjersey. com/coastalcruises) makes boat trips along Jersey's south coast.

Guernsey. Island Coachways (tel: 01481-720210; www.icw.gg) offers half-day coach tours; they also run regular single- and double-decker open-top buses round the coast.

Alderney. The information office can advise on coach and boat trips round the island. For bus tours call ABC Taxis and Riduna Buses (tel: 01481-823760). Subject to sea conditions, *Voyager*, *Lady Maris* and *Alderney Felix* will take you on a 2½ hour trip around the island. The Channel Islands' only train service runs 2–4.45pm, on weekends only Easter to September, and daily during Alderney Week (bookings on: 01481-823580; www.alderneyrailway.com).

Sark. One of the best ways to see Sark is on a 2-hour horse-drawn carriage tour, which can be booked through Isle of Sark Shipping *(see page 125)*. The tourist office *(see page 125)* has information on boat trips round the island.

H

HEALTH AND MEDICAL CARE

The Channel Islands have a reciprocal arrangement with the UK and the Isle of Man under which visitors requiring immediate treatment are entitled to treatment as if they were residents. On **Jersey**, emergency treatment at the General Hospital and appointments with GPs participating in the visitors' scheme are free. You must specifically request National Health Service treatment from the doctor.

The National Health Service does not operate in the Bailiwick of **Guernsey** (i.e. Guernsey, Alderney, Sark and Herm) but UK visitors are entitled to 'immediate necessary' hospital, medical, dental and nursing services and general medical, dental and ophthalmic services. **Alderney** visitors receive free hospital care, but must pay to see a GP, dentist, optician or physiotherapist, and for ambulance services and the services of a doctor in the Accident and Emergency department. A fixed charge is made for prescription drugs.

Repatriation from any of the Channel Islands must be paid for, so even UK visitors may wish to take out health insurance. Visitors are most commonly treated for sunburn – be wary, in the absence of air pollution, the UV radiation is strong.

Hospitals. General Hospital, Gloucester Street, St Helier, Jersey (tel: 01534-622000). UK residents can get free treatment at special morning clinics (May–Sept Mon–Sat, Oct–Apr Mon, Wed and Fri only). The emergency unit is open at all times for treatment, including emergency dental care. Princess Elizabeth Hospital, Le Vauquiedor, St Martin, Guernsey (tel: 01481-725241).

Chemists. The outlets of Boots at 23–29 Queen Street, St Helier, Jersey (tel: 01534-730432) and High Street, St Peter Port, Guernsey (tel: 01481-723565) provide a full range of over-the-counter and prescription medicines. Both open on weekday evenings in summer.

Surgeries. Lists of doctors are available at most main post offices. For GPs in Jersey call: 01534-616833. On Guernsey, visit the Healthcare Group at Pier Steps below Boots (*see above*; tel: 01481-711237; Mon–Sat mornings). For a doctor on Alderney, tel: 01481-822494. For a doctor on Sark, tel: 01481-832045.

L

LANGUAGE

English is spoken throughout all the Channel Islands. Some older citizens may communicate in *Jerriais*, *Guernesiais* and *Sercquais* – the local patois based on Norman French – in Jersey, Guernsey and Sark respectively, but you're more likely to come across Portuguese being spoken by seasonal workers. Most road, street and place names (and surnames) can be traced to Norman French, although they often receive anglicised pronunciation; some street names are bilingual, with the traditional French version appearing alongside the contemporary English name (not a translation).

LOST PROPERTY

On Jersey, contact the States of Jersey Police lost-property department, tel: 01534-612305. On Guernsey, contact the States of Guernsey Police lost-property department, tel: 01481-725111.

M

MEDIA

Radio and television. All national UK radio and television stations can be picked up. In addition, Channel TV broadcasts news bulletins on ITV. BBC Radio Jersey (88.8FM) and BBC Radio Guernsey (93.2FM) are largely talk-based stations, while Jersey's Channel 103FM (103.7FM) and Guernsey's Island FM (104.7FM) play music.

Newspapers and magazines. Jersey's and Guernsey's own daily newspapers, the *Jersey Evening Post* and *Guernsey Press* offer fascinating insights into local life, with reporting, entertainment and gossip. They're full of practical information, including tide, ferry and plane timetables, and the weather. On Alderney there is the fortnightly *Alderney Journal* and Sark has *La Vouair de Sercq ('The Sark Voice')*. The UK's national newspapers arrive by air on the day of publication, weather permitting.

Among the free literature aimed at tourists, Jersey's *What's On* and the fortnightly Guernsey *Holiday Special* offer useful roundups of attractions, restaurants and events.

MONEY

Currency. The Channel Islands are linked with the UK in a monetary union, but the bailiwicks of Jersey and Guernsey each issue their own banknotes (£1, £5, £10, £20 and £50) and coins (1p, 2p, 5p, 10p, 20p, 50p, £1 and £2). English and Scottish currencies are accepted and both bailiwicks accept each other's currency. However, Channel Islands notes and coins are not legal tender in the UK. A growing number of shops welcome payment in euros.

Banks and currency exchange (for opening hours, *see below*). All the major UK banks have outlets in St Helier and St Peter Port (there are some, too, on Alderney and Sark) and provide exchange facilities – as do Jersey's and Guernsey's airports and ports.

Credit cards are widely accepted, though many guesthouses prefer or only take payment by cheque or cash; ask in advance.

Travellers cheques and Eurocheques are widely accepted as direct payment by hotels and by some shops and restaurants.

Value added tax (VAT) does not exist in the Channel Islands. This, and low duty on imported luxury items, accounts for the cheaper prices on many goods. However, because of transport costs, the prices of many everyday items are higher than they are in the UK.

○

OPENING HOURS (See also PUBLIC HOLIDAYS)

Banks. Banks on Jersey and Guernsey open at least from Mon–Fri 9.30am–3.30pm. Banks on Alderney and Sark shut for lunch.

Pubs. On **Jersey**, pubs may serve drinks Mon–Sat 9am–11pm, Sun 11am–11pm. On **Guernsey**, pubs open Mon–Sat 10am–12.45am, and Sun noon–12.45am, when drinks are only served with a meal. **Alderney's** pubs open any time between 10 and 1am. On **Sark** pubs open till 11pm but are closed on Sunday.

Shops. Normal opening hours on the islands are Mon–Sat 9am–5.30pm. On Jersey and Guernsey some 'convenience' stores open on Sunday, some shops close for a half day on Thursday (particularly in winter), and some shops in St Helier stay open late into the evening in summer. On Sark most shops shut for lunch and on Sunday, as is the case on Alderney, which also has half-day closing on Wednesday.

Museums and sights. Closing times indicate when the sight actually shuts: some larger sights refuse admittance up to an hour before the advertised closing time.

P

PHOTOGRAPHY

Camera equipment and digital storage cards are sold in specialist shops in St Helier and St Peter Port and convenience stores throughout the islands. When the sun is shining, brilliant colours make the islands' coastal and beach scenes particularly photogenic.

POLICE (See also CRIME and SAFETY AND EMERGENCIES)

In an emergency, telephone **999**. Island policemen wear uniforms similar to those of British bobbies. These professional officers are aided by an age-old network of elected parish policemen on Jersey, with titles like *centeniers* and *vingteniers*, who enjoy similar powers to regular police officers, but wear no uniform.

POST OFFICES

Jersey's pillar boxes are red, Guernsey's are blue. Each bailiwick runs its own post office and issues its own stamps. Leaving Jersey, mail must bear Jersey postage, and from Guernsey, Sark or Herm only Guernsey stamps are valid. From Alderney, both Alderney and Guernsey stamps can be used. Unlike in the UK, mail is not divided into first and second class. There are three separate postage rates for mail: within a bailiwick, to the UK or the other bailiwick, and abroad. The main post office in Broad Street, St Helier, opens 8.30am–5pm Monday to Friday, and 9am–2pm Saturday, and in Smith Street, St Peter Port 8.30am–5pm Monday to Friday, 8.30am–noon Saturday. Both have a philatelic bureau with local stamps for sale as well as exhibitions, and the post offices on Alderney, Sark and Herm similarly appeal to collectors.

PUBLIC HOLIDAYS

The Channel Islands observe the same legal holidays as the UK plus Liberation Day, commemorating the end of the German occupation of the islands. Alderney had virtually no inhabitants left to be liberated so does not observe this holiday and has a bank holiday on the first rather than the last Monday in August as part of Alderney Week celebrations *(see page 99)*.

1 January	New Year's Day
March or April	Good Friday and Easter Monday
First and last Mondays in May	Spring Bank Holidays
9 May	Liberation Day
Last Monday in August	August Bank Holiday
25 December	Christmas Day
26 December	Boxing Day

R

RELIGION

Each parish has a parish church belonging to the established Anglican Church. Tourist offices also provide details of services for the many other religions represented in the islands.

T

TELEPHONES

Jersey and Guernsey Telecoms run up-to-date, efficient services at relatively low prices (in Guernsey, a local call of unlimited length on a private telephone costs just 5p). Public telephones come with full instructions. In the bailiwick of Guernsey, most take both phone cards and coins (10p, 20p, 50p, £1), while on Jersey phones take only coins or only cards. You can buy phone cards from newsagents and post offices. Calls are cheaper between 6pm and 8am Monday to Friday and at weekends. If you are likely to use a mobile phone, a Jersey Telecom (www.jerseytelecom.com) or Guernsey Cable and Wireless (www.cwgsy.net) pay-as-you-go SIM card might be an economic alternative. The telephone code for Jersey is 01534, and for Guernsey, Alderney, Sark and Herm, 01481.

TIME ZONE

The Channel Islands, like the UK, are on Greenwich Mean Time. Summer Time moves the clocks forward one hour between April and October. Except for a short period around the beginning of October, France is one hour ahead of the Channel Islands.

New York	Montreal	**Jersey**	Paris	Jo'burg	Sydney	Auckland
7am	7am	**noon**	1pm	2pm	1pm	midnight

TIPPING

In some restaurants, a service charge (typically 10 percent) is added to the bill. If not, a tip of at least 10 percent is expected. Tour guides and taxi drivers should be tipped 10 percent, porters in hotels £1–£2.

TOURIST INFORMATION

Jersey and Guernsey operate their own information services in St Helier and St Peter Port. Guernsey's holds some information on Alderney, Sark and Herm, all within its bailiwick, but it is best to contact their offices directly. Channel Island enquiries from overseas are dealt with by British Tourist Authority offices: www.visitbritain.com.

Jersey. Jersey Tourism Visitor Services Centre, Liberation Square, St Helier, JE1 1BB, tel: 01534-448800, www.jersey.com. Open Mon–Fri 8.30am–5.30pm year-round; weekends as follows: Oct–Mar Sat 9am–1pm, closed Sun; Apr–May Sat and Sun 9am–1pm; June–Sept Sat 8.30am–5.30pm, Sun 8.30am–2.15pm. Jersey Tourism has a branch in London for telephone enquiries only: tel: (020) 7808 3822.

Guernsey. Information Centre, PO Box 23, St Peter Port, GY1 3AN; tel: 01481-723552; see www.visitguernsey.com. On the North Esplanade. Open Apr–Sept 9am–7pm, Oct–Mar until 5pm.

Alderney. Contact the Alderney Information Centre, 34 Victoria Street; tel: 01481-823737, www.visitalderney.com; open 10am–noon and 2–4pm; or the States Office, Victoria Street; tel: 01481-822811; open Mon–Fri 9am–12.30pm and 2–5pm.

Sark. For information on Sark, contact the Visitor Centre, tel: 01481-832345, www.sark.info. Located at the top of Harbour Hill. Open summer Mon–Sat 10am–12.45pm, 2–4.45pm; winter hours tie in with boat arrivals. You can also try Isle of Sark Shipping (tel: 01481-724059) on White Rock, St Peter Port, Guernsey.

Herm. The Administration Office, Herm Island, via Guernsey, GY1 3HR; tel: 01481-722377, www.herm-island.com. Open daily 8.30am–5pm all year.

TRANSPORT

Inter-island transport. Services listed below apply only in summer; at other times they are considerably reduced or nonexistent. Consult also companies' timetables and local newspapers *(see page 120)*.

Aurigny Air Services, tel: 01481-822886/8, www.aurigny.com

Blue Islands, tel: 01481-727567, www.blueislands.com

Condor Ferries, tel: 01305-761551, www.condorferries.com

Isle of Sark Shipping, tel: 01481-724059, 24-hour Info Line: 12036 (local calls only), www.sarkshipping.info

Manche Iles Express, tel: 01481-701316, www.manche-iles-express.com

Travel Trident, tel: 01481-721379/722377.

Between Jersey and Guernsey. Aurigny Air Services operates frequent daily flights (15 min duration). Blue Islands has up to nine flights a day. Condor Ferries provides daily catamaran and passenger and car-carrying ferries (1 to 2¼ hrs). They offer day-trips with island coach tours and time for shopping in the ports. All ferry services leave from and arrive at St Helier and St Peter Port.

To Alderney. Aurigny and Blue Islands fly twice-daily from Guernsey and Jersey (20 min). Condor sails from Guernsey (45 min) on Sunday morning only, with a return afternoon boat. Manche Iles Express provides a twice-weekly service from Guernsey. There are no car ferries.

To Sark. Isle of Sark Shipping has frequent daily crossings from Guernsey (1 hr) except on Sunday, when there is only one crossing; telephone or visit their office for advice on advance booking. Ferries from Jersey to Sark (summer only) take 45–55 minutes. Ask at the tourist office for details.

To Herm. Crossings from St Peter Port's various quays take about 20 minutes. Travel Trident has the most frequent sailings, including the 8.30am milk boat (allowing for a very full day on the island) and evening crossings which take in meals at the Mermaid Tavern *(see page 142)*. Advance bookings are not encouraged. An infrequent service also runs from Sark: contact Isle of Sark Shipping for details.

Day Trips to France. (France is an hour ahead of the Channel Islands except between the end of September and mid-October.)

Aurigny flies daily direct from Guernsey to **Cherbourg** (25 min) and to **Dinard** (30 min), with connecting flights from Jersey and Alderney. Rockhopper has direct flights from Jersey, Guernsey and Alderney to **St Brieuc**. Condor operates daily morning ferries from Jersey to **St Malo** (1 hr 10 min), with evening returns. For a day trip to St Malo from Guernsey use Condor; the journey takes 1 hr 45 min.

A 15-minute ferry runs from St Malo to Dinard. For elsewhere, short-term car hire is expensive. The most economical way is to buy a ticket which includes the ferry and coach transport in France.

Buses. Jersey's bus lines radiate from the central bus and coach station at the Weighbridge, St Helier, and **Guernsey's** from the quayside bus terminal in St Peter Port. The services reach most beaches and sights. Island Coachways issues very useful booklets of timetables. Unless you buy a pass or Wave & Save smart card *(see page 109)*, you pay as you get on board. On Guernsey there is a minibus service from Petit Bôt on the south coast to some nearby inland attractions. See www.jersey.com (search for 'buses') and www.visitguernsey.com/gettingaround.

Trains. The Channel Islands' only working railway – which celebrated its 150th birthday in 1997 – is on Alderney and runs from Braye Harbour up to the northeast coast and back again.

Taxis. Taxi ranks are found at the airports, ports and in the towns. If you need to book a cab, consult the *Yellow Pages*. On Jersey try: Luxicabs (tel: 01534-887000); on Guernsey, Fonacab (tel: 01481-232919) or the Weighbridge taxi rank (tel: 01481-714143); and on Alderney, ABC Taxis (tel: 01481-823760).

TRAVELLERS WITH DISABILITIES

Jersey and Guernsey tourist boards distribute good access guides to the islands (Guernsey's includes information on Alderney, Sark and Herm). They include admirably full details on the accessibility of accommodation, transport, sights, shopping, restaurants and toilets. There is a lot of useful information on www.jersey.com (search for 'disabled facilities'). Jersey Shop Mobility provides wheelchairs and scooters to use around town (tel: 01534-739672; www.shopmobility.org.je). Guernsey's Traffic Committee operates a disabled persons' parking badge scheme.

W

WEBSITES

These tourism sites may be useful when planning your holiday:
http://jersey.com
www.visitguernsey.com
www.alderney.net
www.sark.info

WEIGHTS AND MEASURES

The metric system has made some headway in the Channel Islands: petrol for example is sold by the litre. But pints of beer are unassailable and road distances are measured in miles rather than kilometres.

Recommended Hotels

For an overview of accommodation on all the islands and help with reservations, see *page 107*. Book well in advance in summer, especially on the smaller islands.

The price bands below serve as a guideline for the cost of a standard en-suite double room and breakfast for two people in high season (July–August). Prices quoted for Sark and Herm also include dinner for two. Prices fall considerably in the spring and autumn and even further in the winter months for the few hotels which stay open at these times of year. Half-board rates usually offer better value than bed-and-breakfast rates and package costs usually undercut the hotel's own rack rates. If travelling with children, it is worth shopping around; typically the price is half the adult rate if sharing the parents' room, but some establishments are more generous.

££££	over £130
£££	£80–130
££	£55–80
£	up to £55

JERSEY

ST HELIER

La Bonne Vie ££ *Roseville Street, St Helier, Jersey, JE2 4PL, tel: 01534-735955, fax: 01534-733357, www.labonnevie-guesthouse-jersey.com.* Bed-and-breakfast in a Victorian terrace with award-winning garden. Some bedrooms with four-posters; others are small, but there are thoughtful touches in all. Five minutes' walk from the town centre and one minute from beach with tidal pool. 10 rooms.

Eulah Country House ££££ *Mont Cochon, St Helier, tel: 01534-626626, fax: 01534-626600, www.eulah.co.uk.* Former Edwardian vicarage in a tranquil garden setting with lovely views over St Aubin's Bay. Luxurious guest rooms, each individually designed and all with kingsize beds. Upstairs seaview lounge with fully stocked 'Honesty Bar'. 15 minutes walk to St Helier; 5 minutes to the beach. No smokers or children under 14. 11 rooms.

Grand Jersey £££–££££ *Esplanade, St Helier, Jersey, JE4 8WD, tel: 01534-288454, fax: 01534-737815, www.grandjersey.com.* Newly refurbished late-Victorian seafront pile. Several restaurants including the gourmet Tassili overseen by Albert Roux. 122 rooms.

Millbrook House £££ *Rue de Trachy, Millbrook, St Helier, Jersey, JE2 3JN, tel: 01534-733036, fax: 01534-724317, www.millbrook househotel.com.* Peaceful, family-run hotel converted from late 18th-century house, set in 10 acres (4 hectares) of park and gardens. Bedrooms with garden and sea views; public rooms furnished with antiques. 24 rooms, 3 self-catering apartments.

Revere £££ *Kensington Place, St Helier, Jersey, JE2 3PA, tel: 01534-611111, fax: 01534-611116, www.revere.co.uk.* Converted old coaching inn with characterful carved bar and atmospheric, beamed restaurant. Attractive pool and 58 mostly quiet bedrooms.

Uplands ££ *St John's Road, Mont à l'Abbé, St Helier, Jersey, JE2 3LE, tel: 01534-873006, fax: 01534-768804, www.morvanhotels. com.* Modern accommodation based around traditional granite farm buildings. Above St Helier, one mile from the town centre. 43 well-equipped rooms, 12 self-catering apartments.

AROUND THE ISLAND

Beau Couperon £££ *Rozel Bay, St Martin, Jersey, JE3 6AN, tel: 01534-865522, fax: 01534-865332, www.southernhotels.com.* This hotel occupies what used to be an early 19th-century barracks. Its granite walls back directly onto the beach. There's a choice of small but cheerful bedrooms (about half of them with balcony) or self-catering apartments. 36 rooms.

Château La Chaire ££££ *Rozel Bay, St Martin, Jersey, JE3 6AJ, tel: 01534-863354, fax: 01534-865137, www.chateau-la-chaire.*

co.uk. Sumptuous furnishings, luxurious bedrooms and fine French cuisine (reserve) served in lovely panelled dining rooms – all this in a relaxed, secluded Victorian country house. 14 rooms and 2 suites.

Golden Sands £££ *St Brelade's, tel: 01534-741241, fax: 01534-499366, www.dolanhotels.com.* In the centre of St Brelade's Bay, virtually on the beach. Sea-view rooms all have balcony and splendid views of the bay. Good facilities for children. 62 rooms.

L'Horizon ££££ *St Brelade's Bay, St Brelade, Jersey, JE3 8EF, tel: 01534-743101, fax: 01534-746269, www.handpicked.co.uk.* Jersey's top seaside hotel, particularly popular with business people, sits right on the beach. Comfortable lounges and a choice of three restaurants. Excellent facilities include a large indoor pool, saunas, spa and small gym. Many balconied bedrooms (some with plasmascreen TV and DVD player). 106 rooms.

Lavender Villa ££ *Rue a Don, Grouville Bay, Jersey, JE3 9DX, tel: 01534-854937, fax: 01534-856147.* A proudly run, modest hotel with cottage-style public rooms and colourful bedrooms. A small pool and access to the beach across the golf course. 21 rooms.

Longueville Manor ££££ *Longueville Road, St Saviour, Jersey, JE2 7WF, tel: 01534-725501, fax: 01534-731613, www.longuevillemanor.com.* Book months in advance to stay in one of the Channel Islands' finest hotels and reserve a table to savour the islands' most elaborate, inventive cuisine. Beautiful gardens, superb furnishings within the 13th-century house and impeccable service. 28 rooms.

Moorings £££ *Gorey Pier, St Martin, Jersey, JE3 6EW, tel: 01534-853633, fax: 01534-857618, www.themooringshotel.com.* Small, comfortable hotel between Mont Orgueil Castle and the picturesque Gorey Harbour. 16 rooms.

Old Court House Inn £££ *St Aubin's Harbour, Jersey, JE3 8AB, tel: 01534-746433, fax: 01534-745103, www.oldcourthousejersey.*

com. Known as The Royal Barge in the BBC series *Bergerac*, this ancient inn has fascinating bars, serves excellent cuisine – largely seafood – in its lovely beamed dining rooms (reserve) and boasts 9 fetching en-suite bedrooms.

Peterborough House £ *Rue du Croquet, St Austin, Jersey, JE3 8BZ, tel: 01534-741568, fax: 01534-746787, www.jerseyisland. com/staubin/peterborough*. Late 17th-century house in a small cobbled street close to the harbour, restaurants and shops. 14 rooms.

La Place £££–££££ *La Route du Coin, La Haule, St Brelade, Jersey, JE3 8BT, tel: 01534-744261, fax: 01534-745164, www.hotel laplacejersey.com*. Old granite farmhouse, much extended into an impressive hotel. The tasteful public rooms and award-winning Retreat Restaurant are decorated in a country-house style, while the 40 bedrooms, many with terraces beside a courtyard pool, are plush and pretty.

St Brelade's Bay ££££ *St Brelade, Jersey, JE3 8EF, tel: 01534-746141, fax: 01534-747278, www.stbreladesbayhotel.com*. Relaxing resort hotel, only a few steps away from the beach. Two pools within 7 acres (3 hectares) of lovely, well-kept grounds and elegant public rooms. Great for children. Better value on half- or full-board rates. 80 rooms.

Samarès Coast Hotel and Apartments £££ *Samarès Coast Road, St Clement, Jersey, tel: 01534-873006, fax: 01534-768804, www. morvanhotels.com*. Rooms or self-catering apartments overlooking prize-winning gardens. Fine indoor leisure centre adjoining outdoor pool area. Restaurant with view of sandy St Clement's Bay, metres from the hotel. More apartments (up to 5 person) available at their Uplands Hotel.

Undercliff ££ *Bouley Bay, Trinity, Jersey, JE3 5AS, tel: 01534-863058, fax: 01534-862363, www.undercliffjersey.com*. Upmarket guesthouse in a building full of Gothic touches. Peaceful spot, in the lee of north-coast cliffs; garden, pool, home-made English food. 13 rooms.

Recommended Restaurants

We recommend below all sorts of dining establishments, from smart restaurants to welcoming inns and homespun tea shops. Browse through the accommodation section *(pages 128–135)*, as many of the islands' best restaurants are to be found in hotels. Jersey Tourism's *Eating Out Guide* is a useful companion, with a critique of over 170 places to eat on the island. Reservations are particularly recommended for weekend evenings and Sunday lunch.

The price bands below refer to a three-course evening meal (or lunch or tea where no evening meal is served) excluding drinks or tips. Lunchtime dining is usually much cheaper than in the evening and table d'hôte menus are better value than à la carte. Families and those on a budget might head for one of the many pubs providing hearty, inexpensive meals.

£££	over £25
££	£12–25
£	under £12

JERSEY

ST HELIER

Albert J. Ramsbottom £ *90 Halkett Place, tel: 01534-721395.* Seafood menu, including the island's best fish and chips. Superb value. Closed on Sunday.

Bistro Central ££–£££ *9–11 Don Street, tel: 01534-876933.* Parisian-style brasserie with eclectic French menu, situated very close to the town's main shopping street. Also doubles up as a daytime café spilling on to the pavement. Closed on Sunday.

La Capannina £££ *65–67 Halkett Place, tel: 01534-734602.* A seductive, classy Italian restaurant, whose trademarks include veal, roasts, imaginative fish dishes and flambés. Closed on Sunday. Reserve.

Chambertin ££ *20 Beresford Street, tel: 01534-766678.* Elegant bistro serving authentic French cuisine. Closed on Sunday and Bank Holidays.

City Bar and Brasserie ££ *Halkett Place, tel: 01534-510096, www.cityjersey.com.* Contemporary bar and brasserie that caters for all tastes and provides internet access at your table (which is free if you have a meal here). Good cocktails. Open Monday to Saturday.

Gio's ££ *58 Halkett Place, tel: 01534-736733.* Friendly, unpretentious trattoria serving classic Italian fare supplemented by good seafood dishes. Closed Sunday and bank holidays.

Green Olive ££ *1 Anley Street, tel: 01534-728198.* This warm and unpretentious restaurant was winner of the 'Menu de Terroir 2005', which stresses the use of fresh local produce. Inventive vegetarian, seafood and chicken dishes are a particular speciality. Try the crème brûlée with roasted Jersey rhubarb. Closed on Sunday and Monday.

Olive Branch ££ *39–41 La Colomberie, tel: 01534-615993.* Smart, friendly and central Italian restaurant with the only wood-fired oven in Jersey. Probably the best pizzas and pasta dishes on the island. Closed all day Sunday.

Tipsy Toad Townhouse ££ *57 New Street, tel: 01534-615000.* Large bar, centrally located with excellent pub food. Popular on Friday and Saturday nights.

AROUND THE ISLAND

Blue Fish 2 ££ *La Neuve Route, St Aubin, tel: 01534-747118.* A highly popular fish restaurant with marine decor, including a showpiece fish tank with tropical fish and living coral, and a very relaxed atmosphere. Has a large area for outdoor dining. There is another branch at *8–10 West Centre, St Helier, tel: 01534-767186.*

Borsalino Rocque ££–£££ *La Grande route des Sablons, Grouville, tel: 01534-852111.* Vast, smart, upbeat restaurant with a mini-disco. Fish is the speciality of the house, but you can eat virtually what you like. Closed on Tuesday. Reserve.

Castle Green Gastropub £ *La Route de la Cote, Gorey, tel: 01534-840218.* Won the gastropub category of the 'Menu de Terroir 2005'. The best local ingredients given an imaginative twist. Closed all day Monday.

The Drive In Bistro Garden £ *Coast Road, Gorey, tel: 01534-853278.* Newly refurbished. Specialises in local fish and Japanese sushi and sashimi. Children's menu. Good value.

Green Island Restaurant £££ *Green Island, St Clement, tel: 01534 857787.* Informal restaurant five minutes' drive from St Helier and the most southerly restaurant in the British Isles. Serves some of the best seafood in Jersey plus excellent meat, poultry and vegetarian options. The terrace overlooking the sea is practically on the beach (reserve). Closed Sunday evening and all day Monday.

Jersey Pottery Garden Restaurant £££ *Gorey Village, tel: 01534-850850, www.jerseypottery.com.* Outstanding lobster, crab, prawns, asparagus and strawberries served in a lovely floral environment. Open daytime only; closed on Monday. Reserve.

Le Moulin de Lecq £ *Grève de Lecq, St Ouen, tel: 01534-482818, www.moulindelecq.com.* This pub is set in a converted flour mill dating from the 13th century – it still retains the old wheel cog mechanism, which now provides interest over the bar. Mainstream lunchtime and evening pub food. Newly built restaurant adjoins the old inn.

Old Portelet Inn £ *Portelet Bay, St Brelade, tel: 01534-741899.* A vast, fun pub which caters well for families and children, with an arresting dining room in an impressive converted barn. Serves good-value, good-quality and filling pub food.

The Old Smuggler's Inn £ *Ouaisné Bay, St Brelade, tel: 01534-741510.* Series of cosy, beamed rooms with a fun one-eyed pirate motif on the floor. Above-average pub food.

Panorama Terrace Tea Pot £ *High Street, St Aubin, tel: 01534-42429.* For special blends of teas, exotic coffees, scones, cakes and crumpets in a tea room and garden with a view of St Aubin's Bay. Open 3.30–5.30pm; closed on Monday.

Pizza Express £ *La Route de la Baie, St Brelade, tel: 01534-499049, www.pizzaexpress.co.uk.* Good crispy pizzas served in award-winning glass building with panoramic views of the bay.

The Secret Garden £–££ *Gorey Common, Grouville, tel: 01534-852999.* A very popular café and licensed restaurant opposite Gorey Common. Traditional English cooking plus fresh local seafood in a pine-furnished dining room or, in season, a pretty walled garden. Open for late breakfast, afternoon tea and evening meals (in winter, evening meals Friday and Saturday only; closed all day on Monday and Tuesday).

Suma's ££–£££ *Gorey Hill, Gorey, tel: 01534-853291.* Stylish, lively restaurant overlooking harbour and castle, and serving some of the best food on the island. Good-value set lunches.

Village Bistro ££–£££ *Gorey Village, tel: 01534-853429.* Intricate little restaurant with a long-standing reputation for excellent-value seafood and other dishes. Closed on Sunday evening and all day Monday.

GUERNSEY

ST PETER PORT

Absolute End £££ *St George's Esplanade, tel: 723822.* One of Guernsey's top fish restaurants, offering a broad choice of shellfish and other seafood. This is a popular business haunt for lunch. Reserve. Closed on Sunday.

Christies Bistrot and Bar £–££ *The Pollet, tel: 01481-726624, www.christiesrestaurant.com*. The busiest restaurant, bar and brasserie in town, with a terrace for al-fresco dining.

Courts Restaurant ££ *Le Marchant Street, tel: 01481-721782*. Converted backstreet warehouse with a cosy atmosphere and an enormous menu. Eclectic dining choices – from grills and seafood specials, to pasta, bangers and mash, and more. Closed weekend lunchtimes and Sunday evenings.

Da Nello ££ *46 Lower Pollet, tel: 0871-4264438*. Welcoming, cosy and reliable establishment serving Italian food with some French dishes thrown in. Good fish and puddings, interesting pastas. The set menus are particularly good value.

Dix-Neuf £–££ *19 Commercial Arcade, tel: 01481-723455*. A somewhat trendy, multi-faceted wine bar/café/restaurant, ideally located among the town's shops. All sorts of food available, from pastas to scones and from bangers and mash to croissants.

Gover's Restaurant £–££ *2–4 Victoria Road, tel: 01481-714714*. Large, varied but reasonably priced menu; the speciality is *fruits de la mer* but it also offers good vegetarian options.

Le Nautique £££ *Quay Steps, tel: 01481-721714*. A touch of formality in this long-established institution overlooking the harbour. Italian and French cuisine includes fish dishes. Reserve. Closed Sunday, plus two weeks in January.

Simply Ireland ££ *31 Glategny Esplanade, GY1 1WR, tel: 01481-725554*. The name says it all. Booking is recommended for dinner or try a long relaxed lunch.

AROUND THE ISLAND

Auberge du Val ££ *Sous L'Eglise, St Saviour, tel: 01481-263862*. Beams, pine furnishings and inventive bistro food flavoured by fresh produce from the auberge's own herb garden. Also al-fresco lunches.

Café du Moulin £££ *Rue de Quanteraine, Pierre Du Bois, tel: 01481-265944.* Chef and owner Christophe Vincent runs Guernsey's only Michelin-starred restaurant – gained in 2002. Polished, ambitious cuisine, in an old mill in a delightful rural valley. Closed on Monday.

Fleur du Jardin £–££ *King's Mills, Castel, tel: 01481-257996.* Comely 16th-century inn, full of nooks and crannies, serving good, mainstream pub food. Reserve for interesting, varied dishes in the romantic restaurant.

The Hollows ££ *Le Gouffre, Forest, tel: 01481-264121.* Stylish clifftop café-bar-restaurant with stunning sea views and Mediterranean food to match. The ideal place to lunch during a cliff walk.

Longfrie Inn £–££ *Rue de Longfrie, St Peter, tel: 01481-263107.* A large food- and family-oriented pub (with a Fun Factory for children) serving platefuls of pies, steaks and more sophisticated specials. Good value.

Marina £££ *Beaucette Marina, Vale, tel: 01481-247066.* Stylish restaurant, decked out with nautical paraphernalia. Good-value set dinners; popular with the visiting yachtspeople.

The Pavilion £££ *Le Gron, St Saviour's, tel: 01481-264165.* Awarded the Guernsey Restaurant of the Year in 2000 when it opened, run by husband and wife team of Tony and Joanne Leck. Traditional Guernsey bean jar and gold ice cream, made with real gold.

ALDERNEY

Albert House £ *Victoria Street, tel: 01481-822243.* Home-cooked food and real ales in the heart of St Anne.

Gannets £ *Victoria Street, tel: 01481-823098.* Civilised pitstop for every type of food imaginable – from full English breakfasts to lunchtime salads, steaks, and afternoon cakes and teas. Open also Friday and Saturday evenings for more sophisticated dining.

The Georgian House £££ *Victoria Street, St Anne, tel: 01481-822471, www.georgianhousealderney.com.* Genteel hotel known for popular lunchtime barbecues and Sunday brunches in the Orangery or its award-winning garden. Impressive seafood and Sunday carvery. Reserve.

Nellie Gray's £–££ *Victoria Street, tel: 01481-823333.* Fully licensed restaurant and takeaway serving Indian cuisine and a small selection of English dishes.

The Old Barn £–££ *Longis Road, tel: 01481-822537.* Sizeable restaurant and bar with cosy traditional decor inside plus outside dining in the garden. Opens lunchtimes and for afternoon teas. English and Continental cuisine.

SARK

Dixcart Restaurant ££ *Dixcart Lane, Sark, tel: 01481-832015, www.dixcartbayhotel.com.* Imaginative cuisine served in a candle lit restaurant overlooking the gardens. Provides excellent value for money.

Lobster Restaurant at the Aval du Creux Hotel £££ *Harbour Hill, Sark, tel: 01481-832036, www.avalducreux.co.uk.* Renowned for its seafood but serving a range of dishes which can be taken al-fresco on the poolside terrace.

HERM

The Mermaid Tavern £–££ *tel: 01481-710170.* A multi-purpose pub with a snack bar, serving tasty and inexpensive lunchtime and evening barbecues. The evening restaurant is the place to go on Herm if you want grills, Italian dishes and interestingly presented local oysters.

Ship Inn Restaurant ££ *tel: 01481-722159.* Offers inexpensive lunchtime buffets and traditional *table d'hôte* evening meals, including carvery and vegetarian options.

INDEX

Berlitz pocket guide
Channel Islands

Eighth Edition 2009
Written by Fred Mawer
Updated by Hilary Genin
Series Editor: Tony Halliday

Photography credits
All photography by Glyn Genin, except pages
6, 52, 59, 67, 91, 95 by Pete Bennett

Cover picture: 4Corners Images

Printed in Singapore by Insight Print
Services (Pte) Ltd, 38 Joo Koon Road,
Singapore 628990. Tel: (65) 6865-1600.
Fax: (65) 6861-6438

Berlitz Trademark Reg. U.S. Patent Office
and other countries. Marca Registrada

Contact us

At Berlitz we strive to keep our guides as
accurate and up to date as possible, but if you
find anything that has changed, or if you have
any suggestions on ways to improve this guide,
then we would be delighted to hear from you.

Berlitz Publishing, PO Box 7910,
London SE1 1WE, England.
fax: (44) 20 7403 0290
email: berlitz@apaguide.co.uk
www.berlitzpublishing.com